A Boyhood in the Weald

Neil Lyndon

DOWNS COUNTRY BOOKS

For my mother and my brother

© Neil Lyndon 1998

Neil Lyndon has been a professional writer, journalist and broadcaster for 30 years, having begun to write for national magazines and newspapers while he was still at Cambridge. Since then, he has written for almost every 'quality' newspaper and has been a columnist for *The Times* (where he wrote the Atticus column), *The Daily Mail* and *The Sunday Telegraph*. This is his third book. He divides his time between Suffolk, where he lives with his wife Diana and their three children, and Scotland - where he is preparing a book about the 1988 Piper Alpha disaster and the global oil industry.

Cover design: Sue Miller

ISBN: 0 9519876 8 2

British Library Cataloguing-in-Publication Data.
A catalogue record for this book is available from the British Library

Published by DOWNS COUNTRY BOOKS

DOWNS COUNTRY BOOKS is an imprint of
Pomegranate Press, Church Cottage, Westmeston, Sussex BN6 8RH
in association with
Downs Country Magazine, 22 The Alley, Stedham, Midhurst, West Sussex GU29 0NN

Printed by Ghyllprint Ltd, The Ghyll Print Centre, Heathfield, Sussex TN21 8AW (01435) 866211

Foreword

by Colin Dunne, editor, Downs Country Magazine

I knew Neil Lyndon by reputation long before I could count him as a friend. As a columnist on *The Times* and later *The Sunday Telegraph*, and as a contributor to most of the quality magazines and publications, he was well established as a writer of intelligence and wit. I was asked by a magazine to interview him when he became, for a while, the quarry in a sort of reverse witch-hunt.

Let me explain. Neil had written a book, *No More Sex War*, in which he criticised the philosophy of feminism. It was a thoughtful, well-researched and closely argued book, but it brought howling swarms of venomous feminists down upon him. By the time I got to him, he was slightly bruised and wary. In a restaurant near his Suffolk home, however, we rapidly established an understanding, helped along by several glasses of the cheering stuff and some steady masculine chat about cricket. I left thinking what a good chap he was.

What I didn't realise at the time was that this chance meeting was the most wonderful slice of luck. I had just launched *Downs Country*, a traditional countryside magazine for the southern counties, and since this was a one-man operation, with no Murdochian millions behind it, I was desperately searching for articles, writers, anything to give the magazine a touch of quality. The following day I sent Neil a copy. To my amazement and delight, he replied to say that he had been brought up in Sussex and would write me a ten-article series about his boyhood there. When I told him the meagre fee I could pay, he laughed: 'Buy me a pint instead,' he said. Then he corrected himself: 'No, buy me two and I'll be in profit.'

To be honest, I could hardly believe it: a series of articles by a top-class writer. Exactly what my fledgling magazine needed. When the first one came over the fax (on time, of course, and with a casual 'Do what you want with it' scribbled on the bottom), I was overjoyed: any magazine in Britain would have been proud to print it.

It wasn't long before I realised it was even better than that. As each article came in, it began to build into an evocation of boyhood in Sussex in the fifties, with all the fine detail of friends, rivals, sport, girls, his first bike, teachers and village life - a moment in time perfectly recreated.

But there was something else, too. I gradually became aware of a mystery at the centre of this story. Several people had telephoned me to ask about the writer. His memory for detail was exact: Shermanbury where he lived, Cowfold where he went to school, the mischief, the teacher-teasing, his pride in his father's cricketing prowess, his own passion for sport, the children and the teachers, all identified by name. It was all there, and yet no-one could remember him.

'There was no boy called Lyndon there,' one protesting reader insisted.

I decided to ask Neil himself about this extraordinary business. There was a pause. 'I wasn't called Lyndon then,' he said. 'But my real name will be the last word of the last article.' That was the mystery.

As the articles came in, they acquired a tension that wasn't simply in my imagination. The sunlit days of boyhood around his home in Shermanbury and the village school in Cowfold ended abruptly with what should have been a triumph - passing the 11-plus - but it wrenched him away from his friends, a social schism we often choose to forget. Collyer's at Horsham, which should have been a revelation to a boy with his imagination and academic gifts, instead became a nightmare of humiliation bordering on sadism. In the background, slowly mounting, was the disaster that tore his family apart, ending on the day they left, in furtive shame, to find another home, and another name.

I won't spoil it for you. All I can add is that I didn't have to wait until the last word of the last article. Neil was caught out by his own - and his father's - passion for cricket. During this process I had spoken to Trevor Adcock, a man who played club cricket in Sussex all his life and knew everyone who'd ever played the game there. He was adamant: no Lyndons played cricket in the fifties in that area. But, armed with a few basic clues - his father was called Eric, his brother was Ian - Trevor performed a remarkable piece of detective work. He turned them up in his cricketing records: a photograph of his father and, in club membership records, the two sons 'Master I. and Master N . . .' He told me the surname. It was not one which left room for confusion.

I rang Neil. By this time, I was beginning to feel that I was intruding into a shadowy family secret, as indeed I was. Neil said that was okay. What he really wanted to know was what Trevor had said about his father's cricketing ability. 'He said he was a terrific bat,' I replied truthfully.

Neil was overjoyed. 'And he told me your name,' I added. He went quiet. 'What was it?' he asked. I told him, and the silence went on so long I thought he had been cut off. 'I'm 50 now,' he replied in a strained voice, 'and I haven't been called that name since I was 15.'

What he was doing, I then realised, was exhuming family secrets which had been buried for years. It was this underlying drive of emotion of a sensitive man (a description for which he will not thank me) turning out the long-locked attics of his memories that gave the series an underlying drive, of which, in many ways, Neil himself was unconscious. He was driving out old demons. That's what makes it such a remarkable book.

There is another factor too. Diana Maultby, who ran the magazine's office in Stedham at the time, read the articles as they came in. After the third she said she couldn't understand how someone could make what were, after all, everyday events so fascinating. She compared them with other articles which attempted, without success, to do the same thing. The answer was sweetly simple: 'Because they can't write like Neil,' I said, and that's the truth of it.

When the series ended - and, sure enough, there was the very last paragraph ingeniously inverted to end with his real name - Neil sent me a note thanking me for allowing him to write it. I read it with astonishment. It was this series more than anything else which had put my struggling little magazine on its legs, giving it continuity and class. His story had gripped hundreds of readers, and here he was, thanking me. At the same time, I knew what he meant. For him, I suspect, it had been an exercise in catharsis.

In some ways, it was too good for the magazine. When it came to stories about growing up, this was a minor classic, crying out to be published as a book. When I got together with David Arscott, the Sussex writer, broadcaster and publisher, to launch a series of Downs Country Books, we both instantly agreed that this must be the first.

Since the articles had been published, Neil had been in touch with some of his boyhood friends - Ann Burrell, his first girl-friend, now working as a toxicologist in California, David Sawyer, still living in mid-Sussex - and he volunteered to add a last chapter which neatly tied up the loose ends.

In a modest sort of way, *Downs Country* is now established and successful, which leaves me with a debt I can never entirely repay in pints. So I can only say now what I said then: Thanks, Neil Ba . . .

Whoops, nearly ruined it.

A little London boy. The author pre-Weald, in
about 1950.

1

'All this - and Everest, too.'

The headline on the *Daily Express* was the first thing I saw when I opened my eyes. My father was sitting on the bed, holding the paper and grinning triumphantly. 'Look tuppence,' he said. 'Hillary's done it! And some feller called Tensing. On Coronation Day! Would you credit it?'

The steamy riches of fresh tea and frying eggs and bacon filled the caravan. The portable radio was, as always in my father's waking hours and often while he was dozing, crackling and spluttering the news.

'They say it's raining in London,' he said, 'but the big parade will be going on just the same. I hope your Mum and Ian won't get wet. I expect they're in position now. It's a lovely morning here. Breakfast will be ready in a minute. We're going to have such a day.'

He left me to look at the report of the triumph on Everest while he went back to the frying pan on the Calor gas hob. I was only six but I had been reading the papers for two years. It was the only way to keep up with conversation in our house – all sport, politics, showbiz. I am the only person of my age (born 1946) I have ever met who can remember the Helsinki Olympics, the end of the Korean War, the first tour of the Stan Kenton Big Band, the death of Stalin and the return of the young Queen from Africa after her father's death.

Now it was Coronation Day 1953. As Head Boy of the primary school we both attended in London, my brother Ian had been given an LCC ticket on the parade route not far from Trafalgar Square. Bearing cushions, macs and Thermos flasks, my mother was going with him. My father was going to look after me in our caravan in Selsey. Snuggling under the eiderdown with the *Daily Express* and hearing my dad cooking breakfast in our beloved and cosy van, I reckoned I had the better deal.

In the winter 1994 issue of *Downs Country*, Patrick Moore wrote about his adopted home in Selsey and said: 'Of course, we are cursed with a caravan site (what seaside resort isn't?) but it is outside the main village, and is not too much of a nuisance generally.'

That cursed caravan site – where we started taking our family holidays in 1951, 17 years before Patrick Moore came to Selsey – gave me the most precious days of my childhood; gave me my love of the countryside and, especially, of Sussex; gave me my introduction to cricket and swimming and girls; gave me a taste of adventure and danger and, in Chichester cathedral, the beginnings of Christian reverence. Gave me the Coronation Day Fête and the wisest words a father ever spoke to a son. I hope all that might not have been 'too much of a nuisance'.

In 1951, my parents had found 'the van', as they called it, through old friends from their own Midland childhoods who were then running a corner shop in Selsey. They rented it for three weeks that first summer and bought it - for about £15, I seem to remember - at the end of the season. For the following two summers, my mother, brother and I lived in the caravan all through the summer holidays while my father came down from London at weekends and for his own two week break from the accountancy business he ran from our flat in Baker Street. On Friday evenings, as my mother was beginning to call us for bed, he would come bouncing across the rough field at the brass-hubbed wheel of his 1927 Sunbeam tourer; and then he would join us in our cricket match, with a dustbin for a wicket and a Pakistani bat with no springs in the handle and no rubber grip.

He had played for Warwickshire Club and Ground in 1939 and was one of countless legions of men whose sporting career had been reduced to a sigh for what might have been but for the six years of war. He never complained about this: instead, he ruefully admitted that he had spent the last two years of the war flying up and down India playing cricket for the combined services team of which he was vice-captain. He didn't dwell upon the three years before that when he was bouncing around E-boat alley in the North Sea in minesweepers. His professional longings had gone but he was still good at showing a boy how to shape at the ball, and was to have a good ten years of Sussex village cricket ahead of him (another story). On days when he was at work in London and my mother was making meals in the van, my brother and I would wander all over the fields and woods around Selsey with other children from the caravan site. There is a photograph of me, uncomfortably under the arm of a curly-haired five-year-old girl whose grin makes it look as if she saw me as a catch. I do not remember her; but I remember Elizabeth (there were many Elizabeths then), the 17-year old with copper hair who walked with us through the woods one day when the sun was slanting through the trees and picked me up and pointed to a red squirrel in the branches, as electric in colour as she. I did not see another red squirrel for more than 40 years; but I kept looking for a long time for a red-haired girl with soft arms and bare legs.

In a sandy inlet in West Wittering one afternoon, while we were searching for the machine-gun cartridges which still littered the area from the war, I sank to my armpits into oily black sand. My brother hauled me out and was declared a hero by the others who said he deserved a George medal. Instead, he got a Coronation ticket and,

Standing by 'the van' with an unknown admirer: 'a curly-haired five-year-old girl whose grin makes it look as if she saw me as a catch.'

like the rest of us, a mug and a cardboard escutcheon. Heroes and Head Boys had modest expectations then.

After we had listened to the Coronation ceremony on the radio, my father and I had fish and chips for lunch (was there a fish and chip shop in Selsey? Am I making this up?) and a drink in a pub garden before we went to the fête. Where would that have been held? Was there a Vicarage garden? My father threw down Everests of tins with wooden balls and won us a coconut (he never failed in this) and shot the heart out of a playing card with an air-rifle and won us a goldfish in a proper bowl which properly died in less than a week. Then I went in for the six-and-under sprint.

About a dozen of us set off at the whistle, all flying elbows and knees, running up a slight incline over a distance of fifty yards. I was ahead. I looked round to see how far behind they were and tripped on the slope. I fell. They surged past. My father came out of the crowd lined up on either side of the track, wearing a double-breasted blue blazer and grey trousers, holding a fuming Senior Service and he picked me up and wiped my tears away and said: 'Here's a lesson for future life for you, tuppence: if ever you get ahead, don't look back.'

All that and an unforgettable motto, too. When my mother and brother got back to the van, late that night after we had met them off the train at Chichester, they said they had got wet through and hadn't seen a thing. I remember the gas lights sputtering in the van as we went to bed and I remember feeling that I was in the best family and the best country in the world. Millions slept on those thoughts that night.

2

The nine year-old in this house came home from his village school last week breathless with hot news. The father of his classmate Kevin was about to be despatched to Bosnia on a secret mission leading a guerrilla group.

'Ah yes,' I said. 'Isn't this the same man who played for Tottenham Hotspur before he joined the army?'

'That's the one,' said Alex.

'Hmm,' I said and withdrew quietly to my lair, there to reflect on the fragile line – which generations of nine year-olds have trod, have trod, have trod – between the fictions that make you the class hero and the fantasies that every adult can see right through. It was not for me to ask Alex why a man who could play for Spurs should choose instead to become a square-bashing squaddie; nor to say that a guerrilla mission known to every kid in Year Six at his school might not be much of a secret in Bosnia. I was in no position to be superior. Forty years ago, in another age and another village school, I was the Kevin of my time.

In 1953, my parents bought a house in Shermanbury, on the road between Cowfold and Henfield. Though they had never been country people, our blissful summer holidays in the caravan in Selsey had persuaded them to give up their flat in London, sell the caravan and move permanently to Sussex. The great fogs in London in the early Fifties had frightened them and they hoped to give their whey-faced city boys a rosy-cheeked life in fields and woods.

I think, also, that, having a bit of money for the first time since the War, they felt they could afford a step up. At weekends all through the summer of 1953, we toured West Sussex in my father's 1927 Sunbeam Tourer (known as 'Duffy' in our family) looking at houses. My favourites were ancient cottages with thatched roofs and odd-shaped rooms in the eaves. One was on the green at Wisborough Green. Another was near to Chichester. Fifteen years later that house appeared on the front pages of national newspapers when it belonged to Keith Richard, and the Rolling Stones had a party there with Marianne Faithful and a Mars Bar. Ignoring my tastes, my parents kept looking for a house nearer to a main-line station for London and, in September, they found a square three-bedroomed 1930s villa on the ribbon development through the Weald and bought it for, I think, £2750.

My brother Ian was then 11 and I was just seven. They found him a place at Shoreham Grammar School, a private institution with woeful standards, to which he travelled every day on the steam train from Partridge Green station. I was sent on the Number 17 Southdown bus to St Peter's C of E primary school in Cowfold.

My father began a commuter's life on the train from Horsham to Victoria and the office he had taken in Oxford Street, where he was developing an accountancy business for showbiz clients who included, at various times, members of the Ted Heath band and Lita Rosa and the young disc jockey Alan Freeman. My mother stayed home and did battle with the copper boiler in the outhouse where she did the washing on Mondays. The rest of the week, until she crocked her back and we hired a part-time gardener, she wrestled with the lawns and flower beds and 80

F.R. Slocombe ('Old Slokie') in the garden of School House, Cowfold, in 1947 - the year in which he became headmaster of St Peter's Church of England Primary School.

(Photograph courtesy of Mrs Margaret Slocombe)

trees in our long, thin garden running back to an open field and a secret passage through a hedge into an enchanted rookery wood.

My brother and I had been bound together in the same schools in London but our ways parted in Sussex and we would never know each other so well again. His life at Shoreham was a mystery to me, opened only on Sports Days when he won the Victor Ludorum and Prize Days when he got nothing. My Cowfold days did not interest him – which was lucky because I had quickly made them into a gigantic and complex web of fiction, fantasy and downright lies. It would have disintegrated instantaneously if any member of my family had touched it with a prod of enquiry or truth.

St Peter's school must then have had about 60 children under the headship of F.R. Slocombe, 'Old Slokie' to us - a Welshman of fiery ginger brows who had flown as a bomber navigator with the RAF during the War, had been shot down and been a PoW and was still, in the Fifties, I now realise, recovering from the unexpected shock of surviving. He grumpily coked and riddled the iron stoves that burned red hot in winter and complainingly carted in the crates of milk bottles that were our free gift at morning break from a motherly state.

These tasks, he let us know, were hardly fitting reward for a man of his age and history. Between his stories of training in Canada, raids into Germany and escape plots, he taught the senior class and took them up to the 11-plus which Cowfold pupils mostly failed. A very young man named Mr Squires, newly inspired from teacher training and fresh out of Christ's Hospital, took the middle class, divided by an Edwardian partition of oak and glass from the seniors. The infants were in a separate room, under Mrs Luxford, a matronly lady who lived in the village. It was in Mr Squires' room that I found my talents for invention.

All the other children were locals. Their fathers were cowmen on the farms or nurserymen in Lower Beeding. Some worked for local building firms and others in the seed and grain store in the middle of Cowfold where fine dust hung thick in the sunlit air around Foden lorries. Their mothers did not know much about a world beyond copper boilers.

The village of Cowfold today is squarely in the commuter belt and the parents of many of the children at St Peter's - a big and bright primary school with airy rooms - must work in Horsham and Crawley in the modern industries that have been created there. London must be a near annexe to them. Forty years ago, I was not merely the only one at St Peter's who had been born in London and the only one whose father worked there: I think I might have been the only one who had ever been there. I was even more foreign a being to the other kids, and they to me, than a boy born in Los Angeles might be in Cowfold today. We had owned a television since 1950. Many of them had never seen one. They listened to The Archers, Take it From Here, The Billy Cotton Band Show and Journey into Space on the radio. I felt like a creature from another planet.

St Peter's spread before me a *tabula rasa* on which I might compose any story for myself. If I told Colin Sparks that my father had played cricket for England, he could not turn to Wisden to confound me. If I told Barry Harmer or David Sawyer that I had been chosen to captain an England team of five year-olds when I lived in London and that we had beaten Hungary at Wembley, with a double hat-trick from self in the first half before I replaced our injured goalkeeper in the second and kept the Magyar hordes at bay, how could they question the story, even if they doubted it (as they did)?

My father's racy life in London supplied me an unlimited source of material evidence to support my fantasies. His clients and their friends gave him autographs and presents for me and I would turn up at the school gate with signed and personally dedicated photographs of David Whitfield and Joe Loss and of Lita Rosa, hers signed across a saucy decolletage. These were sensational marks of distinction, as covetable as it would be today if a schoolboy could prove to his friends that his dad was on close terms of personal friendship with the Spice Girls.

Barry Austin, who was always grudging in his admiration, said that an autograph didn't count if your father had collected it rather than getting it yourself; but most of the others were regularly stunned and even Old Slokie took a close interest and a lingering look at Lita. My father's disc jockey clients also gave him heaps of unwanted demo discs and we had copies of Johnny Ray and Tommy Steele and Bill Haley before my friends ever heard them on Two-Way Family Favourites. While the other kids read *Dandy* under the desk, I had my father's copy of *New Musical Express* and spoke knowledgeably about new hits recorded by family friends.

This metropolitan other-worldliness ought to have been enough for a little boy at a rural primary school to impress his friends, but my appetites were as boundless as their experience was narrow. My fantasies stretched out into the world beyond the Weald and I saw myself as the conductor of that wider world into St Peter's. Open their minds; give them some excitement; get Old Slokie out of the last war and into the new. Like all vaulting ambitions, mine was finally to be felled by hubris.

When the Suez crisis began and the *Daily Express* carried front-page photographs of the Vulcans flying on their missions from Cyprus, I invented another brother. He was 29 year old and an RAF

'Oakview', the author's boyhood home in Shermanbury.

pilot. He had been promoted pilot of a Vulcans and was stationed in Cyprus. He was a front-line combatant in Sir Anthony Eden's white man's crusade against the Nazi Nasser.

Of all my inventions, this was the most thrilling and the most taxing. Teachers and children wanted news from the front which I would supply at break-times, frantically embellishing the news I had heard on the radio that morning. Had we heard from my brother? The War Office had sent my mother a telegram: he was missing, presumed lost. Why had I never mentioned this brother before? He was so much older than I that we rarely saw him and, besides, his work was top secret, Stupid. What was his name? I think it was Roger.

In any normal month, I might have got away with it. As the only child in Shermanbury who went to Cowfold, I never saw my class-mates out of school and my parents never met theirs. In the weeks of the Suez crisis, however, there was a Parent-Teacher meeting at St Peter's and my father came home early from London to collect my mother and drive her to Cowfold.

I lay in bed, listening to the car coming home. Doors banged violently below as they entered. My mother's feet thundered up the stairs. 'I want a word with you, young man,' she said as she stormed into my room. 'Mrs Luxford came up to me in tears at the meeting and asked me if I had any news of my poor son at Suez. I didn't know what she was talking about. What have you got to say for yourself?'

What she most violently resented – and some violence was expressed on this point – was the idea that she, who was not yet 40, might have a child of 29. My father laughed about this for a week and when the riot had subsided and I was helping him in the garden on Sunday morning, barrowing leaves, he told me, 'Nineteen would have been perfect; but 29 was asking for trouble. If you're going to make up stories, you've got to be very careful with the details.'

I am now hoping that this message might work its way through the decades and the generations to Kevin.

3

Alex played in his first football match last month. It was a five-a-side tournament for nines-and-under in a local village with teams from all around the area. As a disaster, you could call it unmitigated. In my experience, they always are.

Alex and his mates had been practising for weeks in the school playground. What that means is that they had been taking shots at goal, pretending they were Kanchelskis or Giggs, Shearer or Cole and racking up the score. 'I scored eight today,' Alex would say when he came home from school. 'One was a brilliant header. Jonathan Ballantyne crossed and I got up and SMACK! it was a beauty. I think we'll do really well in the tournament.'

The local scrapyard had provided a team strip in emerald green, with the yard's name emblazoned on each little chest. Under the apprehensive eyes of a gaggle of parents, our lot kicked off against a team of aliens from five miles the other side of the river who called themselves the Hornets and were dressed in suitably buzzy stripes. From the off, it was apparent that the Hornets were a tidy, composed team of competent players who knew how to trap, pass, run off the ball into space and hit a shot with either foot.

Our lot were clueless. They all ran together in a bunch wherever the ball went, leaving open space all over the pitch for the Hornets to exploit. They couldn't tackle, head or pass. In defence, they gathered limply around the goal, fearing to approach the attacker and turning their backs to the ball. In attack, they stood and watched while their team-mates ran forward. They were knackered in minutes. Having no team spirit or understanding, they set upon each other with screams of recrimination, while the goals crashed into their net. They were 0-3 down at half time. That was after seven minutes.

I was in such a rage, bellowing instructions and orders from the line, that the other adults edged away from me.

'Get into space!' I screamed. 'For God's sake, mark up!' I yelled.

'You're an embarrassment,' whispered my wife Diana.

I walked away to compose myself, wondering why I should have to turn a village occasion into the last minutes of a World Cup Final. The answer came to me as I smoked a scrounged cigarette sitting under an oak tree: I was still waging the football and cricket wars between Cowfold and Henfield that began exactly forty years ago in 1955 and raged on until 1958.

In the autumn of 1955, Old Slokie's top class at St Peter's C of E school in Cowfold contained a squad of players who considered themselves rivals to Busby's Babes at Old Trafford. Leslie Langridge, Colin Sparks, Brian Newman, David Sawyer, Richard Keane, Barry Austin and I played for half an hour before school started every morning, all through morning and dinner breaks and again in the afternoon. The goal was a stretch of the wall behind Mrs Luxford's classroom. The ball had once been fuzzed with a yellow coat; but if it had ever had a life as a tennis ball, that identity had been rubbed from its surface over years of being kicked and bounced around an asphalt playground and it was now nothing more than a grimy globe of black skin.

Commanding the heart of our team was Barry Harmer, a midfield supremo - we used to call them half-backs - whose control,

St Peter's School, Cowfold.

vision and muscular presence combined, in my eyes, the grace of Johnny Haynes and the authority of Duncan Edwards. His ability to juggle the ball on either foot and keep it in the air on his knees made him a Puskas to me. Better yet, he was my best friend and the only other boy my age who lived in Shermanbury.

'You ought to be playing for England, Barry,' I remember shouting to him one day when we were playing at home. 'I know you will one day.'

Our goal in Shermanbury was a rick of straw bales in the rough field, directly opposite our house on the other side of the A281 from Horsham to Brighton. I was the keeper, imitating Ray Woods of Manchester United (later to be the hapless victim of Peter McParland's brutal charge in the 1957 Cup Final) and spreading myself as broadly as a tubby nine year-old could. Barry was the son of a cowman who lived down the lane behind Miss Hart's Post Office in Shermanbury. His family had moved from a farm near Portsmouth and he was still a Pompey fan, idolising Jimmy Dickinson. I, being already a devotee of fashion and a vessel of cheap sentiment, was in love with Manchester United, as I was to remain for the next 25 years. We both took a dispirited interest in Billy Lane's Brighton and Hove Albion, both knowing, even then, that it was a sure and certain path to disappointment.

Barry had the talent. I had the kit. My father, sparing no expense as was his habit, kept us regularly supplied with leather balls with leather laces and rubber bladders, made in Pakistan and bought from Horsham, which we regularly lost. He had also succumbed to my unremitting pleadings and wheedlings and bought me a pair of Continental boots from the shoe shop in Henfield, probably the first to be worn by a boy in the Weald.

The cobbler and my father had both been reluctant to agree the sale, as if they would be supplying me with an item as potentially injurious to the health of the young as heroin. 'Look at these toecaps,' the shopkeeper sighed, 'No reinforcement at all.' My father shook his head, agreeing, and said 'And these cutaway uppers: look how they expose the ankles. I don't know if you should have these, Neil.' My look of anguish turned the moment and opened his wallet, as ever. 'All the young boys want them,' said the shopkeeper. 'They won't listen.' The boots were mine. They were ox-blood red, the colour of the Magyars, I thought. They had the signature of Stanley Matthews stamped on their side in gold letters. I would have preferred Bobby Charlton's. The old order was changing fast and squirts like me could sense it in their bones.

Barry played in his own father's old boots, laced so high up the shin and so heavy in the toecap that they might have seen service at the Somme. Yearning for 'Continentals' he looked on mine with killing covetousness but said nothing, only whapping the ball past me and thudding it against the straw-bale goal with an envious ferocity. In my new boots, I felt I could lead England, if the call came. With the rest of the Cowfold boys, I felt we were ready for glory. I think it was my idea that we should challenge Henfield.

Assuming the role of team captain without any nomination or election, I put the idea to Old Slokie. His lack of enthusiasm, I now realise, must have been connected with an unwillingness to extend the hours of any working day by supervising a match after school. I nagged and persisted. He gave in and told me to write a letter to the head of the Henfield primary school. I drafted the letter for days, ending up with a missive like an eighteenth-century ambassador's address to a head of state of such grandiloquence and pomposity that - the Henfield kids later told us - the whole school had collapsed in laughter when it was read out in assembly.

The reply came speedily and curtly. The Henfield captain said they would be glad to take us on, after school on the following Wednesday, on their village pitch beside the cricket ground.

The problem of a team strip preoccupied me. We had none. No local firms were then in the business of sponsoring kit. No team in the country was then merchandising replica strips. None of the other boys had indulgent fathers with cash to spare. What could we wear? I hit on white shirts - we all wore them to school - and black shorts, which we could all scrounge. We spent all our time arguing about this problem and about the positions we should play. We should have been practising.

We took the Number 17 Southdown bus from Cowfold to Henfield at 3.45 on that October afternoon, changed in the cricket pavilion and took the field about 4.15. By 4.16, we were a goal down.

Henfield, having kicked off, had moved the ball rapidly upfield with a series of crisp passes through our chaotic defence (where was Barry? where was the supremo?), finally reaching their captain on the edge of the penalty area. He slipped past a feebly extended Cowfold leg (it was probably too heavily booted to lift) and essayed a shot at the goal I was guarding. I dived. The ball went beneath my body. I would say - I did - that it bounced wickedly before me. In truth, I think, it went straight along the ground. It went in .

Slokie groaned from the touchline and put his shining head with its ginger tufts of hair in his hands. The team remonstrated. I lay in the mud, wanting to die.

'I've never played in a goal this big,' I complained.

'We're all in the same position,' said Barry. 'None of us has ever been on a pitch before.'

It was true. The scale of the Henfield pitch and the size of the goals dwarfed and overwhelmed us. Our opponents spread out comfortably and took their ease of us, spraying passes and raining down attacks in practised formations. Shots bombed in on me from all sides. High and low, straight and crossed, they all went in. We were five down at half time. Nine at the end.

Slokie was so enraged that he didn't speak to us on the bus, nor for days after. We had disgraced the school and him, he finally let us know. The following Wednesday afternoon, instead of putting us through his RAF-inspired PT routines on 'the apparatus' in the playground, he marched us up to the Cowfold playing field, over the road from the village hall, and organised team practice. I was not in goal. Peter Spedding, even more mountainous than I, took my place. Slokie saw me as a barging, bashing centre forward after the style of a Ron Flowers or Nat Lofthouse, with no natural gifts but plenty of weight. That was to become my role for the rest of my footballing life, until girls and fags destroyed my fitness and supplanted my passion for the game around the time of my 16th birthday.

Throughout the winter, the training continued. Slokie was grim, remorseless. We ran and tackled and harried under his bombardier's bellowing until our legs fainted. In the Spring, he sent a letter of challenge himself, inviting Henfield to our patch.

They came with rampant cockiness and condescension. We took

them apart. Barry roamed the field like a Beckenbauer, seizing the ball from their indecisive grip, demoralising them with his vision and his passes. Colin Sparks, at inside-right, was a terrier, whipping the ball through their defenders. I was banging it in, two before half-time, a third in the second half. We scored six. They got none.

Old Slokie was a changed man at assembly the next day. Beaming broadly and showing his pipe-stained teeth, he regaled the school with the story of our heroism and the best result ever achieved by Cowfold against Henfield. We could all hold our heads high, he said. 'Cricket practice will begin in the first week of the new term,' he concluded. 'I shall be sending Henfield a challenge during the Easter holiday.'

The wars were on.

Christmas at Cowfold School.

4

Praise be, the ordeal is over for another year. It is not the buying and the wrapping that exhaust us, nor the feasting, nor the family spats. We collapse with a sense of relief that we have ticked off another trial and that there can be, at most, only another nine seasons of Christmas concerts and carol services to suffer before all our children have grown beyond them. Another generation of parents will then be condemned to sit for hours on December evenings in chilly churches and on school chairs like anvils, smiling grimly through half-hearted renditions of *Good King Wenceslas* and muttered, stifled readings of the story of the three kings.

Alex, the ten year-old, is worth watching on these occasions for giving the best artistic impression of somebody who is not really there. He dwarfs himself in the back rank of the chorus, sinks both hands in his pockets and opens and closes his mouth, soundlessly. Between songs, he and his friend J. Ray compete to give the most polished exhibition of their most advanced talent - synchronised yawning and nose-picking - rushing to the doors for release at the end like lifers completing their term.

At the bottom of their boredom, I think, is a fathomless ignorance. Our kids and all their contemporaries have not the dimmest glimmer of understanding of these ceremonies. They are uninstructed heathen, as baffled and mystified by Christian ritual as the children in the opening scene of *The African Queen*, wailing their cacophonous hymns under the despairing instruction of the missionaries, Robert Morley and Katherine Hepburn. The 'godhead veiled in flesh' means less to them than $e=mc^2$. Their schools have thoroughly eschewed Christian indoctrination in favour of a more liberal-minded muddle.

When Isla, the twelve year-old, does her RE (I think it means Recreation and Entertainment) homework in this house, we find her puzzling over food-chains and family trees. Divinity does not even enter the margins of these tasks. She could no more name the books of the Bible than she could decode Stockhausen. Hers must be the first generation of British children for 1200 years who couldn't hazard a guess why Joseph and Mary had to go to Bethlehem. This is not a joke.

Whether it matters or not is another question; but I can say with absolute certainty that things have changed beyond recognition. In the Fifties in the Weald, Old Slokie's class at St Peter's C of E school in Cowfold approached the Christmas festivities with the disciplined religious sensibilities of a band of Jesuit novices; and we sang in church - or he would want to know the reason why, and would enforce the question with his bamboo cane - like the massed ranks of the Huddersfield Choral Society. With Slokie scowling watchfully from the pews, you missed a note or picked your nose at your peril.

Whether F.R. Slocombe was, himself, a believer I have no idea. He did not discuss his beliefs with his brats. A Welshman by birth, he was probably Methodist by upbringing. As the headmaster of a Church of England primary school, however, he had duties to his governors to conduct religious education according to a specific and, at that time, changeless order, and he executed them with the unbending seriousness of a Cranmer. His war years in the RAF had given him a settled belief in the benefits of drill and he applied it to all his teachings, whether of arithmetical tables or of liturgy. Repetition, chanting, repeated rehearsal, constant practice were the watchwords of his methods; and they lodged in his pupils' minds - or at least in this one - ineradicable, lifelong certainties. I can bring to mind the words of the Apostolic Creed as easily as I can say the twelve-times table. Both were embedded there under the martial arts of Slokie's choleric, fuming, impatient instruction. You couldn't get them out now if you used hot tongs.

I cannot say it was much fun. Old Slokie did not go in for jubilation or religious ecstasy. Our fifteen-minute morning prayers were funereal, even with jolly old Mrs Luxford striking up the hymns on the joanna in the corner of Slokie's classroom.

Friday mornings brought an extended ordeal, when Slokie tuned to the BBC's Schools' Service on the ancient radio in its walnut cabinet that was connected to a loudspeaker hanging on the wall in a plywood box, where it gathered dust beside a framed photograph of the young Queen. The broadcast was a full morning service, with sermon, during which somebody - usually Richard Keene or Brian Newman - always got found with a *Wizard* or a *Hotspur* under the desk and was sliced three times with the cane across the hand by a splenetic Slokie as soon as the service had ended and while the valves were still cooling in the radio.

Most unendurable of all, however, was Mr Parr's Thursday morning hour's drilling in the Catechism, a word I cannot hear even now without a chill of dread seeping through my veins (not that you're ever likely to hear it round this house).

Mr Parr was the vicar of St Peter's church in Cowfold and chairman of the school's governors. It was his solemn duty to give weekly instruction to the top class and prepare us for the confirmation that every one of us, I suppose, expected to receive. A thin, tall, stooped, shy and reticent man, with an almost hairless pink pate - though he cannot have been more than 35 - he brought to his lessons as much colour and vivacity as he wore in his dusty black cassock with its thin and frayed brown leather belt.

He should have been awarded a black belt and bar in boredom. No adult has ever been more adept at stupefying a classroom full of ten- and eleven-year-olds. His method of instruction was to have us learn the Catechism by heart, line by line, response by response, page by page, until we could say every word of the whole thing.

And he wasn't quick about it. A full hour might be taken over the following peppy exchange:

Question: What is required of persons to be baptized?

Answer: Repentance, whereby they forsake sin; and Faith, whereby they steadfastly believe the promises of God made to them in that Sacrament.

The Ten Commandments might have taken a morning for Jehovah to relay to Moses but they took us a month to get by rote to Mr Parr's satisfaction. All eleven sentences of the catechist's declarations of 'duty towards my neighbour' were so irremovably imprinted on my brain that, when I came to swear the Cub's promise in the Scout Hut in Henfield in 1957, I found myself better prepared to swear to 'keep my hands from picking and stealing, and my tongue from evil-speaking, lying and slandering', as the Catechism requires, than promising 'to do my best', as Baden-Powell had ordained.

Having begun the course in September, Mr Parr's target was to complete the Catechism by July so that leavers of Cowfold school should go forth armed to meet the heathen foe in the sinful world. At the beginning of the next school year, he started again with 'What is your name?' Those of us who were in Slokie's top class for three years were thus under continuous instruction in the rite for what felt like an aeon of eternity.

As soon as Mr Parr entered the classroom, Slokie exited, saying that he needed to catch up on his paperwork. Retreating to his little office by the girls' cloakroom, he helped himself to a pipe and lost himself in the morning newspaper. We could see him through the glass partitions. He emerged only when Mr Parr lost control of Brian Newman's or Richard Keene's attention - a twice-weekly event - and the din of disobedience in the classroom broke his concentration on the crossword. He would then burst in - his red cheeks shimmering with fury, his ginger hair alight on his balding scalp - and, ignoring the hapless Mr Parr, inform the boys what they would get as soon as he resumed teaching; but they already knew that. After Mr Parr's visits, the palms of boys' hands were regularly as bright with raised blood as Old Slokie's cheeks.

Even if he was not a catechist, believing 'all the articles of the Christian faith', Slokie sure believed in the power of song. We chorused more often than we prayed, and not just hymns.

On Tuesday afternoons, Slokie tuned the radio into the Schools' Service again for a singalong programme, complete with rudimentary musical instruction in crotchets and quavers, which we followed in a BBC booklet. 'Now we'll all turn to page 11 and sing together On Richmond Hill', said the nicely spoken man on the radio. 'Eleven, you nitwits,' roared Slokie. ('It's easy work being a teacher if all you have to do is switch on a radio,' muttered Yvonne Childs, who shared my desk.)

On Friday afternoons, before school ended for the week, we had an extended rehearsal with Mrs Luxford at the piano for the following Tuesday's programme. Slokie put us sternly through these rehearsals as if he was determined that we should not disgrace ourselves in performance with the rest of the nation in earshot.

Through that programme and Slokie's regimental diligence, I learned a hay-wain full of the folk songs of the British Isles that are with me still. Those Wealden kids would bellow forth with 'Marie's Wedding' as lustily as 'To be a Farmer's Boy', with 'Men of Harlech', 'The Raggle-Taggle Gypsies' and 'To Be a Farmer's Boy' as loudly as 'Hearts of Oak'. I have never had more pleasure in music than I got from those hours, though the pleasure in music they started in me has never waned.

Rehearsals for the Christmas carol service started in October, immediately after half-term. The Trooping the Colour could not have been more scrupulously prepared. Slokie was possessed with the performance, I suspect because he liked to show poor Mr Parr how a body of children could behave if they were properly disciplined by a man who had known war.

He picked the members of the choir with more care than the teams for the Cowfold-Henfield cricket and football wars. The chosen twelve, six boys, six girls, had to learn parts and harmonies and descants, anthems and solos. We also had to learn how to process up the aisle behind the vicar, dressed in surplices; and we had to master an ornate, Slokie-choreographed routine for ushering the girls first into the choir's pews. The boys led the girls, all in step, up the aisle. At the altar, the files parted and the boys stood back in line to let the girls go first. At the end of the service, therefore, the boys again led the girls out of the pews and down the aisle.

The symmetry of this dance was particularly important to Slokie and he cared about its perfect execution as much as the Lord Chamberlain preparing a march of the Knights of the Garter. Every year the choir went to the church to practise for five mornings before the service. Every year some hapless novice to the ranks of the choir would foul it up, going first into the pews before the girls and breaking the pattern of the ranks for the return procession; and every year, at the morning prayers on the day after the service, Slokie would go berserk, asking God Almighty himself what he had to do to get a simple instruction obeyed by pudding brains.

'Next year, we'll start rehearsals in September,' he would bellow.

In my last year at Cowfold, when I had been singing in the choir for three years and was its elder, Slokie chose David Durrant to join the choir for the carol service for the first time. It fell to David, therefore, to err in the dance and enter the pew before the girls. I could see Slokie throughout the service, glowing like a lantern of rancour in the pews of the congregation. David Durrant was so ashamed and frightened, knowing the wrath that would soon descend upon his head and his hand, that he couldn't sing a peep.

At the end of the service, as we rose to follow Mr Parr down the aisle, I stood back and let the boys and girls out of my pew, tagging onto the end of our file and pairing up with David as he emerged from the opposite side, restoring an odd but pleasing symmetry to the march.

Old Slokie, seeing this, lit up his face with a beam of pure radiant joy. I never saw him so enraptured. He rushed to my mother as she was leaving the church to congratulate her on having a boy so full of brains and sense. He shot into the vestry to pump my hand while we were changing out of our surplices. At prayers next morning, he lauded my name as if I had won an Open Scholarship to Oxford. For the rest of the term - two days - I could do no wrong.

I am glad our kids are spared the boredoms and the pains of the F.R. Slocombe instructional methods in music and religion, but I could wish they had received the benefits. The chief of those now seems, perhaps oddly, to have been the communication of a certain sense of place. Those drills in our country's songs and its articles of faith cemented in us a concrete sense of belonging, just as surely as Old Slokie's geography lessons - in which we had to build Plasticene models of the Weald and the Downs, with all its geology in coloured layers and its woods and streams and iron works in place. They let us know where we were and they connected us with our parents and with their parents, all of whom had received the same instruction and knew it in their bones.

No child at St Peter's in the Fifties would have pretended not to be there when we put on our performance for the parents at Christmas. Fearing Slokie as much as the God of wrath, none of us would have dared. The result was that we really were there – in heart and spirit, as much as in voice and harmony.

5

'You know what, Dad? You're useless at this game.'

The second time my son John saw me with a cricket bat in my hand, he was eight, I was 44 and my middle stump had just been smashed.

A 17 year-old in our village had asked me to go over to the nets on the rec to check his bowling action. I had been giving him tips since he was 10 and now, standing more than six feet and weighing more than 12 stones, he was one of the best club bowlers round our way.

Far too good for me. With the sun glowering redly behind his shoulder, he bowled to me off his full 20-yard run, accelerating towards the bowling crease in the rhythmic approach we had created together (an imitation in my mind of the fluid graces of Lindwall, Trueman and Michael Holding). Supposing he was still the boy and I the master, looking to impress my own son who was standing beside the net, I played forward to his first ball, was beaten for pace and bowled middle stump. The stump splintered.

Something else was flattened in that instant: it was that dangerous, addictive fiction that goes mutually between a father and a boy under ten, the one that says the old man can do anything if he puts his mind to it - swim the Channel, make a million, score a hundred. The first time a boy sees his Dad play cricket must be like the first time a stone age boy watched his father go hunting, seeing him as a man among men, following men's pursuits. John had forgotten the first time he saw me play and would always carry the memory of that shattered stump as his first, disenchanting, initiation. The first time I saw my father play was more like how it is supposed to be.

It was at Henfield in May 1954. My father, Eric, had joined the club during our first winter in Shermanbury. In conversations in pubs and with his commuting companions on the trains from

Horsham to Victoria, he had carefully sorted out the qualities of all the local clubs and had ruled out most of them. If a village club cared nothing about the state of their wickets, didn't dress uniformly in whites or allowed fielders to smoke in the field, my father would not want to sully with them the only love I think he ever took seriously, the love of cricket.

He was 42 (so I was seven). He had not played the game since VJ Day marked the end of his idyll in India, where he was vice-captain of a Combined Services team and spent the last two years of the war flying up and down the sub-continent, playing three-day games against maharajas' teams (I once asked him how close he came to the enemy during those years and he said 'About 1500 miles, I should think. Your mother was in far more danger living in London.') Now he was looking for a local team that did proper honour to that loveliest and most intelligent of all ball games but was not so good he would embarrass himself. Horsham were too good for him, he reckoned; Partridge Green were too rough and amateur; Henfield were perfect. They had a good wicket; an orderly pavilion; sightscreens, a scoreboard with rollers and a scorer (what a scorer!); and nets with concrete and matting pitches.

I went with him to some net practices on Friday evenings in the late Spring of 1954. He wanted to find his eye again and he wanted to test the team's bowlers. He was impressed. A man named Trevor Adcock played for the club. He wore the scarlet cap with crossed golden sabres of Steyning Grammar School and was a medium-pace swing bowler of real, testing talent and guile. Something tells me he was left-arm: I wish I could check that memory with my father.

I do remember that Trevor Adcock fooled my old man several times in the nets and rapped his pads and was congratulated by my father who would say 'Good ball' and pick up the ball in his gloved left hand and throw it back to Trevor with a rueful smile.

Other of the village bowlers he drove and pulled and hooked and glanced with growing confidence and power and I saw them exchanging glances and heard them whispering 'He knows what he's doing, all right, don't he?' At the end of that first session, the Henfield captain asked my father to turn out for the team in the next Sunday match but he said he would need some more nets before he played in a match. It was another three weeks before he went in at number six on a Sunday afternoon against - can this possibly be true or am I guessing? - Poynings.

He had always been a natural number three or four; but he had chosen to bat lower in the order that day because he did not want to push himself forward. He also told me 'By the time I get in, with any luck their good bowlers will be finished.'

I watched from the boundary, sitting on the grassy bank, high up by the A281, where the Number 17 Southdown bus used to stop. An ice-cream van was selling drinks and I had mystified the driver by asking for a bottle of 'Zup' because I couldn't see that this lemonade new to me and Britain was called 'Seven-up'. And then, when the old man walked out to the wicket, I was more nervous, aching for him to do well, than I have been when my own child has performed in public.

He played himself in carefully, opened his account with some comfortable ones and twos and then he let them see his favourite stroke of all. I can see it now. Facing the bowling from the pavilion end, he was given a short ball rising outside the off-stump. Stepping back and turning his wrists, he clipped the ball with a perfect flicking square cut and sent it skittering low to the boundary, where I joyfully collected it and threw it back to the fielder.

He had scored 19 and two wickets had fallen when his tail-end partner called him for a suicidal single. Responding to the call without complaint, my father set off but, no Jesse Owens, he had made only two-thirds of the pitch when the wicket was broken. He saluted his partner, in a gesture of condolence as much as of forgiveness and walked briskly back to the pavilion, receiving respectful applause.

Later he told me he had been glad to go for the run, knowing he would be run out. 'I was already tired and losing concentration,' he said. 'If I had batted much longer I might have thrown my wicket away. It looks better this way.'

At Wisborough Green, two weeks later, he scored his first 50 for Henfield, including a stepping-down-the-wicket six picked up on the half-volley and struck straight over the bowler's head and the sight-screen. I strained my tonsils yelling: he told me not to be so demonstrative. Now his eye was properly in and he had the measure of most bowlers he was likely to meet on the circuit of Sussex villages. Still going in at five or six and declining promotion, he ran up regular, weekly, 30s and 40s and was top (or second, I'm not sure) of the club's batting averages at the end of the season. When Henfield had their annual meeting in the autumn, they invited him - as I had predicted - to become vice-captain for the following season. I was officially allowed to go in the scorebox and work the rollers.

I was already possessed by the game. On my tenth birthday in September 1956, while I was eating my mother's trifle and watching Eamonn Andrews interviewing Len Hutton on Crackerjack, my

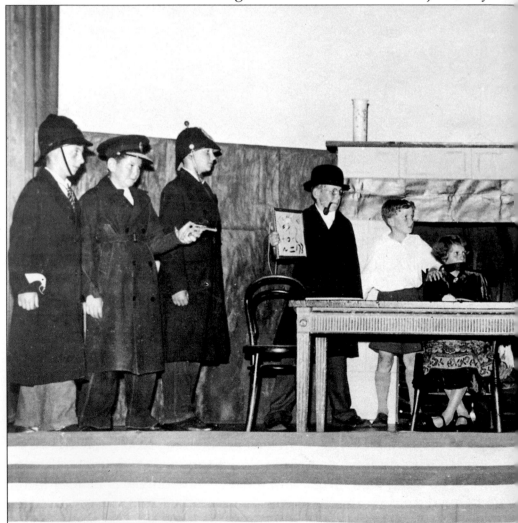

father asked 'Would you like Len Hutton's autograph?' For a boy of that age, this was like asking if he might like to receive the keys to Paradise. My Dad left the room and returned with a copy of Hutton's autobiography *Just My Story*, signed for me by every English schoolboy's ultimate hero, the Swan of Pudsey and captain of the first England team to recover the Ashes for 21 years. On the day of publication in May 1956, my father had queued for two hours at Foyles to get Hutton's autograph on his book for me and had kept the present for four months until my birthday. Showing off my treasure at school, I felt as proud of my father as I was of Hutton's signature.

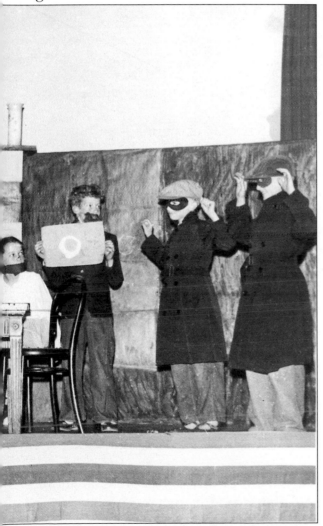

St Peter's School play, June 1957, directed by F.R. Slocombe. The author is seen with his father's pipe and a borrowed bowler. Other cast members include Ann Burrell *(seated, centre)*; Leslie Langridge *(with a hand on her shoulder)*; Barry Austin *(with beard and painting)* and Richard Keene *(far right)*.

It would be good to get the Henfield club's records now and check this, but I am pretty sure they were a classy side in those mid-Fifties, capable of testing any of the touring teams containing has-been county players who regularly came for weekend matches. I don't remember ever seeing Henfield get slaughtered or tossed out for fewer than 30 runs, routine experiences of my own village cricketing years. I am sure my father's judgment of Trevor Adcock was right. I have never seen a cleverer, subtler all-round village cricketer. A prolific scorer and wicket-taker, he was also a blinding cover-point, in the manner of Colin Bland. He often pretended to fumble the ball, encouraging the batsmen to go for a run and then he would whip the ball in to the keeper over the bails with a throw as true as a stone from a catapult.

Those records of Henfield in the Fifties must exist somewhere. They were compiled by a scorer named Pam who was one of the reasons why my mother called a halt to my father's village cricket career around 1957 or 1958.

Pam, who never missed a match, was about 28, I suppose, and she worked in a bank in Horsham. A single and unattached working woman of that age was a rarity in that decade and Pam was viewed with suspicion by the cricketers' wives and with some lewdness, which even a boy could pick up, by the men themselves who talked about her while they were putting on their pads or applying their Elliman's Rub.

Pam's morning bus to work in Horsham also took me to school in Cowfold. She would ask me to sit beside her in the front seats on the upper deck, where I would sniff at the exotic odours of her face powder and her cigarettes while I answered her questions about my father.

What made me tell my mother that Pam had asked me, one morning, 'How old is your mother?' I must have known that no good would come of it for any of us. 'Bloody cheek!' my mother exploded. 'She can get her hooks into somebody else's husband if she can't get a man of her own. There will be fewer gins for her in the cricket club after this.'

Innocent as I will bet they were of any active misdemeanour, my father and Pam kept their distance after my mother's eruption and I think some of the pleasure went out of my father's cricketing weekends. In any case, the club's matches and nets and social evenings took more time than he could spare. He left home before 8.00 every morning and never got home before 6.45. He brought work home every weekend, did all the heavy work in the three-quarter acre garden and tried to play some golf. I often wonder how he did it all.

By the late Fifties, when he was in his own mid-forties, my father was feeling he had had enough. He gave his solid leather cricket hold-all to my brother and kept his buckskin boots with their studded leather soles for me to grow into (I wore them until I was in my thirties). He reserved his cricketing interests for watching Test matches on television and coaching me and my brother in the garden.

When I was 11 and still at St Peter's primary school in Cowfold, I was asked to play for the village team in a match against Lower Beeding. My father was dubious, fearing that the rough wicket would give an uneven bounce and that I might take a ball in the face and be put off the game for keeps. But he let me play and drove me to the Lower Beeding field and was watching there when I went in to bat in my first men's match at number nine.

He was sitting in a deck-chair on the boundary at about mid-wicket. I was delivered a full-toss down the leg side, inviting a hook which had already become my favourite shot. I saw myself hitting the ball over the boundary and into my father's lap. I saw myself hitting the biggest six a boy had ever struck on that ground and hearing the men say to my father 'That boy can play'. I swung. I missed. The swing carried my bat onto the bails and I was given out for having broken my wicket. First match, first duck.

My father did not tell me until the year before he died in 1989 that I was not out. 'You can't be given out for hitting your wicket if you haven't effected a shot connecting with the ball,' he said. 'They didn't know any better.'

In cricketing matters, I have unconsciously but unfalteringly followed him. In 1984, I took a lucky opportunity to get Bob Willis's, Ted Dexter's and Alec Bedser's autographs on a copy of Willis's book for my son John. As he was only 18 months old at the time, the gift did not mean a lot to him but I felt I was carrying on an important tradition. Later that summer, he saw me play cricket for the first time, his buggy parked on the boundary while I batted in the middle.

He has no memory of one of the best innings I ever played: the massive six I hit off the middle of the bat, five inches from the toe (I just went to finger the mark on my old bat in the corner of my room) that went over mid-on and through the tops of the alders and into Mrs Graham's vegetable garden; the off-drive off the back foot that streaked across the grass and clanged into the roller. I scored 44 and was out only because I was too knackered to lift my bat and run another 22 yards. I ran myself out, calling for a run that only Jesse Owens could have completed.

That was the day he ought to remember, not the moment he saw my middle stump explode. But the gift of timing, that supreme cricketer's touch, was not given to me as it was to my father. Perhaps all sons would say the same.

6

We have had a quiet couple of weeks in this house on the romance front. After an orgy of dalliances, a frenzy of infatuations, none of our pre-teen and just-teenage kids is at present 'going out' with anybody of the opposite sex. So far as I know. No promissory notes pledging deathless passion have been discovered in shirt or skirt pockets on their way to the wash. We have been spared the protracted glooms and huffs and the venomous, splenetic outbursts which routinely attend the romance gone wrong. Also absent have been those unexplained and unexpected days of gaiety and abandoned laughter that are the sure marks of a fresh fancy. The children are their more normal and singular selves, distant, uncommunicative, mysterious. We don't ask; they don't tell.

'Going out' is a mystery in itself. It doesn't mean that they go anywhere with each other or meet after school or have a date. It doesn't seem to mean that they kiss or take off any of their clothes (but what do I know?). It seems to mean that, in the eyes of the rest of the world and for a moment that might be a morning or a month, they are coupled. Then they 'dump' each other. No very hard feelings go with the dumping nor any very deep devotion with the 'going out'. Easy come, easy go: these courtships look like a rehearsal not so much for a lifetime of marital fidelity as for habitual promiscuity.

Well, drawing up the full weight of my middle-age, I am here to tell you it wasn't like that in the Fifties when I was at St Peter's C of E primary school in Cowfold. When we twinned our souls, we committed ourselves for keeps. There is a little corner of my soul which still feels married to Ann Burrell, though it is nearly 40 years since I duped Old Slokie, the headmaster, and won Ann Burrell for my girlfriend.

It took guile and detailed planning to get through to the girl at all, even though we were in the same year in Slokie's top class.

Unlike the unrestricted and open contact enjoyed by boys and girls today, there was little or no connection between the sexes at St Peter's. We kept to ourselves and we were kept apart as if we might be mutually contagious. The girls had their secret places that were forbidden to us – not just their cloakroom and toilets (strangely known as 'the offices' at St Peter's) but also their own half of the playground and their own entrance to the school. We lined up in separate files to walk to church or to go to games and we sat separately in the canteen for our school dinners and at our desks in Slokie's classroom (how I came to be sitting beside Yvonne Childs for some time is a mystery to me now: perhaps we were immune to each other). We filed separately into church and sat in pews divided by the aisle.

Boys might talk to girls walking to school or, after school, at the bus stop for the Southdown Number 17 that took children north towards Lower Beeding or south to Shermanbury; but we divided at the moment we passed through the Victorian iron railings and gates and barely a word might pass between us for the rest of the school day.

Talking *about* girls being easier than talking *to* them, we did as much of the one as we did none of the other. Between Colin Sparks, David Durrant, Peter Spedding, Richard Keene, Barry Austin, Jimmy Hawkins, Doug Barrett, David Sawyer, Leslie Langridge, Barry Harmer and me there raged a continuous assessment and debate about the qualities and the characters of the girls at school. High on the agenda for this debate were always the ravishing Hawkins girls, Jimmy's sisters, not least because he had seen them without their clothes and was always willing to convey the picture in words. This was the nearest that the debate came to a material rather than a hypothetical reality. For those of us like me, without sisters, the idea of female nudity was so exotic and remote that the clinical photographs in a medical dictionary at home were unbearably exciting. And if we caught sight of a Masai woman's nipple on Armand and Michaela Dennis's 'Safari' programmes on television, we would discuss it, huddled together in the corner of the playground by the coalsheds, for days.

In the years after the War, it was impossible for country boys to find a photograph of an unclothed woman on sale anywhere, so

most of us had no idea what one might look like. Even *Health &
Efficiency*, the naturalists' magazine which occasionally circulated in
grubby copies through our hands, covered the nakedness of its
models, men and women, with gauzy patches of airbrushing.
Salacious interests were absolutely forbidden for boys.

In 1957, I was expelled from the Henfield pack of Cubs for
pinning a photograph of a fully-clothed Kim Novak, torn out of
Photoplay, on the tentpole at camp on Hayling Island. That photograph might be thought a bit too dull for Page Three of a parish
magazine today. The Queen probably wears fewer clothes for a State
Opening of Parliament than Kim was wearing in that fatal photograph.

Anyway, back to Burrell: in the midst of all this puritan repres-
sion and denial, shot through with the coarsest boyish lewdness, I
conceived a romantic longing of the purest ardour for Ann Burrell.
She was the daughter of a nurseryman in Lower Beeding. Her best
friend at school was Beryl Smith.

Beryl was big, hearty, dark and pigtailed. She might have gone
on to become a PTI in the SAS. Ann was slight and slim, almost
translucently pale, with blonde hair in a bob and blue eyes. She was
quiet, watchful, undemonstrative, studious and thoughtful. Ann and
Beryl were the cleverest girls in Slokie's class and they and I always
got the top marks in tests. In 1958, we were to become the only three
from Cowfold in living memory to pass the 11-plus and be accepted
into local grammar schools without a preliminary interview. We had
already become a kind of threesome when I devised a plan to make
me and Ann a twosome.

I had watched her from afar in the playground and had marked
her out for mine. She was the prettiest, the brightest and the most
female of the girls in the school: the others (apart from Janice
Hawkins, for whom we let go a sigh even now) were most like boys.
Consulting a runic astrological book in my parents' slim library, I
had established that Ann Burrell and I were fated to be together (I
don't exactly remember the method by which this book was
supposed to predict your future but I do remember that, if you asked
the same question often enough, it ultimately gave you the answer
you wanted.)

'Does Ann Burrell fancy me,' I asked the charts.

'Like crazy,' it answered (or something like that).

'Will she marry me?'

'You will be together for ever.'

'That'll do,' I thought.

But how was I to contrive to get into her company for any length of time? We were never together for a moment. In the three years we had shared in the same class, I doubt if we had spoken three sentences to each other. I couldn't send her a note: too crude, too obvious, too chancy; she might be embarrassed, she might not reply. I couldn't ring her up: she wasn't on the phone. How could I do it?

I had plenty of time to wrestle with this problem as I lay in bed on early summer evenings in 1957. My mother sent me to bed at 7.30 in those days and I would lie in my room, on a metal box-frame bed, listening to the rooks gathering in the wood beside the house. Like any other boy of that age, in the hours before sleep I read the *Hotspur*, *Wizard* or *Boy's Own* or to wrestled in imagination with airborne Huns. Having read Paul Brickhill's biography of Douglas Bader about three times before I was 10, I was adept at converting my bed into the cockpit of a Spitfire or a Mosquito and flying it in combat over the Channel or on low-level bombing missions seeking out Hitler's Lair.

When the bed wasn't in the air, it was under water and I was a submarine commander on a mission to sink the Bismarck in the North Atlantic. And when it wasn't being a plane or a ship, the bed became Stirling Moss's Mercedes 300SLR, winning the 1955 Mille Miglia. Busy bed.

It was there, between missions and races, that I laid the plan to dupe the headmaster and get the girl. I remember clearly how the idea came to me in stages during one evening and, when it was all in place in my mind, I knew it would work.

I executed Stage One the next morning when I left a note on Slokie's before assembly. He read it out after prayers.

'I have had a most intelligent suggestion from one of the boys,' he said. 'Neil has written to me to suggest that we should have a Suggestions' Box in the school and any pupil who has an idea to improve our lives here can pop a note in the box.'

My reading of Slokie's character had been correct. He was a military disciplinarian; but he was also a sceptic and an individualist. He liked to impose authority but bridled to submit to it. A Suggestions' Box would both allow his children a measure of participatory democracy and would confirm his powers, since he would choose whether or not to implement the Suggestions. He fell for it, in other words, like a ton of bricks.

The poor sap made the box with his own hands, crafting it out of pine that he sawed and planed and jointed and fitted with a hinged lid and screwed to the end of the big bookcase in the top classroom (is it still there?). We kids drew a notice that was pasted above the box, illuminating the word 'Suggestions' with an arrow pointing down at the letter-box slit in the lid.

Slokie put the box in place about a week after I had suggested it. I put the first suggestion in the box about five minutes later, having written this second note at the same time as the first. Slokie again made the announcement after prayers.

'Neil has come up with a marvellous suggestion as the very first idea out of the box,' he beamed. 'He suggests that it would be a good idea, to help me and to encourage a sense of responsibility among the pupils, if we had a Head Boy and a Head Girl.

'I fully approve of this idea,' he went on, 'and there is no doubt at all in my mind who should be our first Head Boy.'

High-flying love: Ann Burrell leaps the bar on sports day, watched by the author's father. She went on to set a county record for high-jumping.

He looked at me, bestowing the gift, with the kind of elder statesman approval with which Winnie might have passed the Tory Party leadership to Sir Anthony Eden. I blushed and looked at the floor.

'Have you any suggestion, Neil, for the girl who might be by your side as Head Girl?'

'As a matter of fact, Sir, I can think of one girl . . .'

Ann Burrell was mine. In the bag. We were as one. Slokie had anointed us.

We were girlfriend and boyfriend for aeons. It might have been a whole school year. It might have been more. Everybody knew. We became an item, a fixture. So far as I remember, we were the only couple in our school. None of the other boys could figure out a way to get at the girls. Beryl and Yvonne were peeved. Ann was queenly in her distinction.

My mother heard about it somehow and got worried. 'You and Ann,' she said 'you're nothing more than good friends are you?'

'Well,' I said, 'we are a bit more than that.' I couldn't tell her that I considered myself as much married as she was.

Thirty years later, I was to hear a similar exchange when my six year-old son was discussing Kylie Minogue with his mother. He, being smitten with the Aussie midget, had put up a poster-size photograph of her in his bedroom (if Kim Novak had been wearing as little as that, my mother would have deprived me of more than my woggle). His mother spoke kindly to him about 'Your friend, Kylie Minogue.'

'Kylie's not a friend,' he hotly answered. 'Kylie's a Love Woman.'

'Hah!' I thought. 'A lot you know. Ann Burrell was a Love Woman and I had to beat a grown man to get her.'

7

Alex's bike is lying on the privet hedge. I hurled it up there five minutes ago. He was watching as I picked it up by its handlebars and frame and, in the action of a hammer-thrower, lofted it five feet on top of the hedge. I suspect my face might have been purple with fury. Alex laughed. He didn't care.

We have been warning him *for years* not to dump his bicycles outside the front door. Nothing we say makes any difference. He still comes hurtling down our track, slides to a skidding halt on the gravel in front of the house and flings his bike to the ground by the door-step. It might stay there all night. He doesn't notice if it lands on its gears. He doesn't think about people trying to get in or out of the door carrying shopping bags or wardrobes and entangling their feet in his bicycle. I'd told him that, next time I tripped over it, I'd throw it in the well; but I threw it on the hedge instead. He thinks this is funny.

He doesn't really seem to care about anything. He can lose a new football the first day he's playing with it and let it go with a shrug. Pens, knives, shoes, clothes, toys disappear without a thought or a care. I gave him a new pair of football boots for his birthday last September and he'd lost them within six weeks. I told him he couldn't have a new pair. He didn't mind.

His mother and I talk about this a lot. We can't understand it. We both remember losing things in childhood and being racked by grief, guilt and fear. Diana didn't sleep for days when she wrecked her new umbrella, as her father had predicted she would, by constantly twizzling it until its bones warped and broke. When I was nine, I was distraught, inconsolable when the fountain pen my father had given me went missing from my desk in old Slokie's class at St Peter's C of E school in Cowfold (I always suspected Richard Keene, Brian Newman or Stuart Faires had half-inched it). My sobs disturbed our morning prayers. The only time we have ever seen

Alex in this state was when our dotty Dalmatian, his special pet, bit a walker outside the house and we said he would have to be put down. Alex's unassuageable grief was one of the factors that spared the beast.

Alex's attitude to material possessions reminds me of a story told by Eddie Fisher after Elizabeth Taylor left him to marry Mike Todd. Fisher had given her a socking great rock of a diamond for her Christmas present, busting the bank to buy it. Twenty minutes after Taylor had unwrapped the bauble and cooed upon it, Fisher saw their kitten playing with the diamond on a rug.

Alex is like that. His mother says it's because children now get so much that they attach no special value to anything. He mystifies me most in his way with bikes. In the last six years, since he learned to ride two-wheelers, I can remember him cleaning his bike once. The nearly new mountain bike he was recently given by a neighbour is mouldering in the garage with punctures in both tyres and, rather than fix it, he borrows his mother's or an adjustable one of mine.

I can't come to terms with this degree of difference between the ages. The bicycles of my childhood in Sussex were such treasures and they took such a massive role in my existence that they were holy to me. They had spirits with which my spirit communed so that I was part of them and they of me. I tended them and kept them with the kind of ceaseless reverential care that old ladies devote to cleaning the church and arranging the flowers. In all my 50 years, no absorbtion, no work, has ever given me more pleasure than I had as a boy when stripping, cleaning, oiling and reassembling my bikes. The scent of Three-in-One oil on the chain was as heady to me as the linseed I put on my bat and the dubbin on my football boots. But, of all things, my bike was sacred, the thing I could not have lived without.

For a child to be given a new bike in those Fifties in the Weald was as rare and as far beyond the expectations of most children as it would be today if a primary school child had a new laptop computer. My brother Ian, who was four years older and was the direct heir to the post-war austerity through which my parents and the whole country lifted themselves, never got one. He had to make do with old heaps my father picked up from auctions and second-hand notices in the shops of Partridge Green and Henfield. I was the beneficiary of their increasing prosperity as the Fifties turned towards the Sixties. Every time I grew out of my bike, my father had the money ready for a new replacement.

On my fifth birthday, they gave me a Gresham Flyer tricycle. In a deep red like the benches of the House of Lords, it had gold coach lines and, of all enrapturing things, a boot with a hinged lid and a chromed twist-handle, behind the saddle. Prince Charles himself was not more fortunate.

My first two-wheeler was a Phillips roadster. I think it cost £12 12s 6d, much more than a week's average earnings at the time. Having written to all the manufacturers demanding brochures, I had been pondering the choice for months, taking the catalogues to bed, reading them over breakfast and under my desk while Slokie hammered the sums and tables on the blackboard. My study was intense, unremitting, as I deliberated over Rudges and Raleighs, sifting the virtues of Humbers and Dawes.

The Phillips to which I repeatedly returned was the acme of cool, though that word had not appeared in the vocabulary of Wealden eight year-olds. It had the straight handlebars which were then a sensational innovation; but it also had whitewall tyres and white mudguards, set against an ice-blue frame, the same colour scheme as the Nash convertible. They called it Palm Beach, whatever that might mean. Colin Sparks said I was just dreaming if I thought I would ever get a bike like that.

On Christmas morning 1954, I went down our chilly stairs to the kitchen for breakfast. I opened the door into the snug fug made by frying bacon and the glowing coal stove. My parents and my brother were waiting, beaming, and there - strike my eyes - was the Palm Beach roadster, with ribbons on its bars and bell, leaning against the kitchen table, so magnificent and glittering I hardly dared touch it.

A 20-yard stretch of concrete path ran from the oak double gates of our house to its rear (we called it 'the drive'). My parents and my brother spent most of that Christmas morning and Lord knows how many hours and days thereafter running me up and down that strip while I tried to balance on the two wheels. We progressed to the footpath that ran through Shermanbury alongside the A281, down to Miss Hart's post office opposite the Partridge Green road. Still, I couldn't get it. My brother and his friend Johnny Goldfinch took it in turns to run and puff behind me along the farm road that went down from the post office and grew irritated with my hopelessness and they told my mother that every other child might do it naturally but I never would. And then, that amazing, unexpected day, I was off on my own and sailing past the pond towards the farm, with the white-wall tyres humming over the gravelled track. Of all the physical firsts of childhood - first swimming strokes, first goal, first kissing, first banana - that first moment balancing on two wheels is the only one I can still feel if I put my mind to it.

The A281 was a fast and dangerous road and I had already come close to death upon it, running across the road to play football in the opposite field with Barry Harmer, directly in front of a car whose driver was white with terror after he had skidded to a halt and got out to remonstrate with me.

Our wire-haired terrier Bunty, my special pet, was run over on that road less than a year after we got her. My parents told me about the catastrophe when, instead of letting me catch the bus home, they came to collect me from school in Cowfold, in the 1939 Rover 14 Sports saloon (FLN 993) which my father had bought to replace his Sunbeam tourer. My wailing and sobbing on the musty green leather seats in the back of the car made my father cry and he begged me to try to stop for his sake. That was the first time I ever saw him with tears on his face and I was so shocked that I did stop. I would not see him cry again until I was 14. That crushing grief over the dead terrier came back to me when I saw Alex hugging the condemned Dalmatian and begging us to spare his life and, being a boy again in him, I knew we could not do it.

Anyway, the road was dangerous and my parents forbade me to ride my new Phillips on it. I had to stick to the footpaths and the farm tracks through and around Shermanbury. That was okay so long as I was small and my strength couldn't carry me far beyond the hamlet's limits. My friends in Cowfold were too far distant then to visit and my brother and I were happy to be confined in the fields around Shermanbury, where we fished in the Adur and the farm pond and went birds' nesting (God forgive us for all the eggs we stole) through the woods and copses.

As the end of my years at St Peter's approached, however, I yearned to stretch further and ride the roads to Partridge Green and Cowfold and Henfield and beyond. My parents' prohibitions became confining. The Weald and the Downs we could see from our house stretched invitingly beyond Shermanbury and, growing tall and, strengthened by Slokie's martial instruction in games and PT, I again needed a bigger bike.

The 11-plus was looming. By 1958, the education authority in West Sussex had changed its line of approach to this test. The old days had gone when the examination was fixed for a date known in advance by all the terrified kids who would have to sit it. Now, we would be put to the fire without notice.

Thus it happened that, one morning in early Spring, Slokie told all the younger children in his class to clear off to Mr Spedding's classroom, leaving behind all of us in our last year. Slokie said he was giving us a test. We looked quizzically at each other, not sure whether the moment had come. I think we had two papers, one before and one after the morning break. I do remember that Yvonne Childs tried to look at my paper over my shoulder while I was writing. Even after we had finished, we still could not agree whether or not we had finally endured that long-dreaded moment of transition, the one that would determine the rest of our school life.

After it was over, we put it out of minds. The cricket season was coming and our school team was, Slokie conceded, the best since the War. I persuaded a carpenter in the builder's shop along the path from the churchyard to make us a heavy block of oak with three holes for sticks to pass as stumps, so that we could have a proper wicket on the asphalt playground. Slokie admired this invention so much that, at the end of the term when I wanted to take it home, he insisted on keeping it for the school's use, scorning my claims that it was mine. If I grit my teeth, I can say I hope it gave many years of pleasure.

After the exam, ages seemed to elapse before, one June morning, an official letter arrived from the council offices in Chichester. My father having already left for work in London, my mother opened the letter while we were having breakfast. She couldn't understand it.

'I think they're saying that you've failed the 11-plus' she said, giving it to me. I looked at the lines of blue type on the stiff white paper with a crushed heart until I said, uncertainly: 'No, they're not. They're saying I can have a place at Steyning Grammar or Collyer's in Horsham. That must mean I've passed.'

'Let me look,' she said. 'Oh, my love, I think you're right. I think you must have passed.'

She hugged me and laughed and cried. In all our family, on both sides, only Auntie Else and Uncle Jack's son Keith had ever passed the 11-plus and my Mum was always in competition with Auntie Else. Over her shoulder I could see my brother near the kitchen door, going out to get the train to his rotten private school in Shoreham. I felt his misery, even in my ecstasy. Four years earlier, he had failed. I felt he would never really forgive me for passing.

I took the letter to school and showed it to the kids in the playground where it instantaneously forced a permanent separation between me and my friends. It quickly emerged that I was the only boy to have had one, but Beryl Smith and Ann Burrell had received the same notice. Barry Austin, David Sawyer and Richard Keene had been invited for interview at the grammar schools. A few weeks later, they too would be given places.

Slokie was beside himself. 'We've never had so many successes,' he chortled through his moustaches. Colin Sparks and Doug Barrett were brave in their glumness. 'I want to go to Steyning Secondary Modern, anyway,' said Colin 'I want to go with my friends and, in any case, I want to work with my Dad on the farm.'

A chill separation set in between us at that moment and lasted until we left St Peter's.

When my father came home that evening and read the letter, he said I should have a reward. I could have the bike of my choice for my twelfth birthday in September, when my new life would begin at the grammar school.

It was decided that I should go to Collyer's in Horsham because the bus went that way from Shermanbury and my father drove there to get the London train, so I could sometimes go with him. The most fateful decision of my early life, one that would bring me years of suffering after the happiness of my childhood education with Slokie in Cowfold, was thus taken for reasons that had nothing to do with education. My parents could not have known better. They sent me to Collyer's as an act of trust, as we all, blindly, submit our children to that unknowable, incalculable future and trust them to the care of strangers we cannot influence or control.

On our last day at St Peter's we parted wordlessly and without ceremony, scattering through the gates at the end of the day, not realising that this was a moment of everlasting consequence. After that day, after all our years of play together at St Peter's, I was never to see Colin or Doug, Barry Harmer, David Durrant, Yvonne Childs or a dozen other friends. Our ways divided forever.

The summer of 1958 was the happiest of my childhood. My family was optimistic and secure and we seemed well off. My parents bought a huge new Frigidaire to stand in the pantry, a 17" Ferguson television with ITV (a first for the area) and a washing machine instead of the old copper boiler in the outhouse. My brother went to Belgium on a school trip and my parents took me to Cornwall for our summer holiday, where I spent all my time practising my fast-bowler's run on Saunton Sands, imitating Fred Trueman and Ray Lindwall. One evening, my parents came back along the sands from their evening walk and my father had a word with me. They had been talking about my future, he said.

'You've said in the past that you might like to be a teacher or a journalist when you leave school,' he said. 'Well, now you're going to the grammar school, you might have a chance. So I want to tell you that it doesn't matter if you don't get there, but you've always got to try for the top. If you're going to be a teacher, you should make it your ambition to be the headmaster of Eton. If you're going to be a journalist, you should want to be the editor of *The Times*.'

Neither of us could have imagined what a laughable mess Collyer's was about to make of those dreams.

Throughout that summer, I was obsessed with the new bike. The brochures arrived by every post and piled beneath my bed. I read them constantly, memorising pages of detailed specifications. I had already won the battle with my father to have a bike with drop handlebars but he was intransigent on the derailleur gears I wanted, insisting that they were flimsy and 'continental' (that was the attraction) and that I should settle for a three-speed Sturmey-Archer hub gear. It was the same argument we had fought over 'continental' football boots and it had the same result. Knowing that he could never win a war of attrition, I kept after him week after week until he submitted. 'That boy can wind me round his finger,' he complained to my mother.

By August, I had settled the choice. The most overwhelmingly glamorous, irresistible bike in the catalogues was another Phillips, a masterpiece of Reynolds tubing with lightweight hubs and derailleur gears they called the 'Fleur de Lys'. It was magnificent in French imperial red and black with gold badging. It cost £30, a breathtaking sum to ask of a parent, perhaps equal to about £450 today. My father hemmed and hawed and said he didn't know. My brother was indignant even to hear the price mentioned. 'The most you've ever spent on a bike for me is six pounds,' he justifiably complained. 'I've never had a bike with one gear, let alone five.'

On my birthday, Ian himself delivered the Fleur de Lys into my hands, wheeling it out from the garden shed where it had been hidden overnight after spending a week under wraps in Mr Knight's filling station down the road. 'Happy birthday,' he said, as my hand took the place of his on the Brooks No 17 saddle, a strip of hardened leather as narrow as a stiletto. He said the words like a threat and we both knew then that he would never forgive me.

'Enjoy it, you deserve it,' said my Dad.

'Don't go too fast,' said my Mum.

And I was gone. Down 'the drive', through the gates, off towards Henfield and Small Dole and Upper Beeding, the Phillips clicking through the gears and humming through the sunshine of my September birthday afternoon, with the Downs, the coast and new life before me. That afternoon, with that first ever grown-up bicycle, marked the opening of adolescence and the beginning of independence. It was the happiest day of a childhood that had been long and rich in happiness; and it was also the last.

Though I had only begun to sense them at Collyer's, shades of the prison house were closing upon me.

8

In the summer of 1958, a merry boy, tubby but tall, used to get off the Number 17 Southdown bus in Shermanbury every afternoon, wave goodbye to his friend Keith, the young conductor who looked like Marty Wilde, and walk home along the footpath through the oak and hazel trees. As he walked, he always whistled the folk and traditional songs he had learned at school, with extra volume for 'Richmond Hill', 'Hearts of Oak' and 'To Be a A Farmer's Boy'.

He would stop at the gates of the first bungalow along the path and a young dog, a tan retriever cross-breed, would fly from the back-door to meet him, followed by the two ladies who lived there. The boy and the dog nuzzled each other, while the ladies asked for news of the boy's day at school. 'We always know when you're coming,' they would say, 'because we can hear you whistling from the bus stop.' After a few minutes, the boy would walk on a hundred yards to the gates of his own home, where his mother would have tea waiting on the kitchen table.

That boy, overflowing with cheerfulness as much as with tune, was me, coming home from Cowfold, where I was in my last summer term at St Peter's C of E primary school. Having passed the 11-plus and won a place at Collyer's grammar school in Horsham, I was looking forward to my coming life with bursting optimism and appetite.

Some disquiets about Collyer's had already been edged into my mind by Tony Brooks, a pale and cunning 13 year-old who had recently come to live with his mother in Shermanbury and was then approaching the end of his second year at the school. The same bus that took me to Cowfold in the morning carried him on to Horsham and we sat together for 10 minutes every day. I was flattered to get the friendship of this older boy, with all his knowledge and experience of the world I was about to enter, in the uniform I was soon to wear.

Neil Lyndon

In the sidelong way he had with a confidence, Tony told me that the few Cowfold boys who got through their 11-plus were not highly regarded at Collyer's. Some of the teachers mocked them as country clods and Mr O'Connor, one of the maths teachers, especially enjoyed running them down. Cowfold boys tended to be placed in the C stream when they entered Collyer's and, if they failed to get promoted to the B and A streams before the end of the third year, they were condemned to the poorest teachers for non-academic

The entrance to Collyer's School, Horsham.

subjects like Technical Drawing. 'I expect you'll be all right because you got through without an interview,' Tony said. 'They should put you in the A stream or the B stream at worst.'

In August, my mother took me on the bus to Horsham to kit me out for Collyer's, an afternoon of massive pride for us both. No midshipman joining his first ship could have been more thrilled than I to finger the gold braid on the blazer's badge or to settle and straighten that first cap on my head. Only the best would do for my mother - the most expensive choices of shirts and gym shorts and worsted trousers. We tottered home from the bus laden with bags, and I spent the rest of the afternoon dressing in my uniform and wore it to tea.

In the last week of the summer holiday, at the beginning of September, the new boys were summoned to Collyer's to meet the headmaster and be introduced to the school. We Cowfold boys went up together on an early afternoon bus, Barry Austin, David Sawyer and Richard Keene joining me on the upper deck of the bus, all in our pristine caps and blazers. In a knock-kneed group tightly bound by nervousness, we walked down Hurst Road to the school and through the main door for the first time. The school's hall alone seemed larger than all of St Peter's and the 90 new boys gathered there were half as many again as all the children at our primary school. Daunted and overwhelmed, we stood silently together until a stunning voice bellowed 'Silence' and the hall was stilled for the entrance of the Headmaster and his deputy. They were Mr Coulson and Mr Wilson.

They strode in majestically. They wore dark suits and regimental ties under scholastic gowns, such as we had never seen. Their appearance confirmed that we had been far removed from the homely and amiable scruffiness of Old Slokie's top class but were now in the presence of commanding professionals. Mr Wilson, a short, taut man of soldierly gait and stance ordered us to sit on the floor and then D.J. Coulson stepped forward to address us.

I remember no words of welcome nor anything kindly in his dark and jowly face, only a forbidding mien and words of warning and admonition. We were, he said, joining a school of proud traditions, high achievements and strong disciplines where we would be required to conform and perform. He explained that we would be divided into streams, each under the control of a form teacher, and assigned to houses with house masters. He read out the names of the boys who would join the A stream. Mine was not among them, nor among the Bs that followed. All we Cowfold boys were placed in the C stream, under Miss M.E. ('Min') Young, the only female teacher on the staff.

We all knew what it meant. We looked at each other, knowing we had been condemned.

When I got off the bus in Shermanbury, my father was waiting for me. His welcoming smile vanished when he saw my face. 'No good?' he asked. I explained. He said it didn't matter. I knew it did.

When we passed the gates of the bungalow on the path going home, the retriever-cross came running from the door, barking and snarling. She did not recognise me in my uniform and took me for a stranger. She never came to greet me again and I am not sure that I ever whistled up that path in all the years I was at Collyer's.

Having been lavished with praise and encouragement by Old Slokie at Cowfold, I had learned to see myself as having some talents and some brains and, enjoying the work, did well. Within a term and a half in lc at Collyer's, I knew that I was thick and began to conduct myself accordingly.

Other new boys in my class, like Stewart and Brand (on entering Collyer's we were reduced to our surnames) had been to prep schools in the area and had already encountered Latin and French. Our teachers G.E.G. ('Gedge') Hunt and 'Mungo' Park made no allowance for the country boys to whom these subjects were as remote and baffling as astro-physics. Old Slokie had drilled us well in our tables, in long division and multiplication, in fractions and decimals, and we were better educated in those skills than Eton boys might be today. But other new boys in lc had already been introduced to rudimentary algebra and geometry and Mr O'Connor took pleasure in deriding our struggles to catch up .

Slokie had taught us brilliantly about the history of our own place, about the Weald and the Downs, about the hedgerows and the fields, the enclosures and the farming methods, about charcoal smelting and iron making. I remember his lessons today, 40 years later. In lc, however, Min Young began our history lessons in Assyria and Persia. I remember nothing she taught us. Miss Young, a dessicated stick of a woman who wore 30 denier stockings in Florence Nightingale shoes, insisted on being called 'Ma'am' and was vexed when, out of years of habit, the Cowfold boys called her 'Miss'. She smiled upon the boys from the Horsham families she knew.

Collyer's was nothing more than a small-town provincial grammar school but it affected the style and the ways of its social betters at public schools. It had house prayers and games and a CCF, as if it thought it was Lancing College. Prefects wore gold tassels on their caps and had unquestionable and arbitrary powers of punishment. They would give 'lines' for minor infractions and 'merit marks' - black marks - for greater offences. If you got three merit marks in a week, you were in detention on Saturday morning. D.J. Coulson was a splenetic and venomous flogger who lashed little boys' bottoms with whimsical unpredictability. The staff, I now realise, was largely composed of second-raters, duds and time-servers who may have resented their own failure to find advancement in grander institutions and took out their bitterness on the boys.

They were irrational in their prejudices, inflexible in their intolerances, ludicrous in their snobberies. It quickly became impossible to admire them. One day, for instance, I remember Mr Davies, the head of the English department, smartingly and loftily reproaching my friend Dennis Strudwick for saying 'eether' rather than 'eyether'. I went to the library and checked the Oxford Dictionary, which gave both pronunciations as correct. When I told Mr Davies, he said 'The Oxford Dictionary is wrong.' Another time, G.E.G. Hunt accused me before the whole class of having copied an essay on Richard II from a book. My friend Barry Austin defended me, saying that I was capable of such work. Hunt would not hear it. 'If he can write that well,' he said, 'he should not be in this class.'

'We all know that,' said Barry.

No satisfaction was to be had at that school except the pleasures of battle. Between the condemned of the C streams and the lower orders of the teaching staff who were condemned to teach them, a state of near-war raged. We new boys quickly picked up its routines and its tactics and, applying ourselves to those plans rather to our homework for which we got no reward, we were expert in the field before the end of the first year. The teachers' chief function was to impose maximum humiliation, pain and misery on us; ours was to torment them beyond endurance and to get away with it.

Some master mischief-makers quickly appeared among us. Tim Hurst and Kurt Holt, the only black boy in the whole school, had a touch of genius in their strategies for driving Fred Bennett, 'Frog' Kenyon and George Henderson up the wall. At the top of their form, they could make those men hysterical in minutes. The success of their plans depended on split-second timing and uniform obedience from the rest of 1c, which the teachers could never command.

Frog Kenyon absent-mindedly picked his nose, his index-finger buried knuckle-deep, while he sat at his desk and we were supposed to be poring over our books. One day, he looked up to see 30 boys looking back at him with their fingers up their nostrils.

George Henderson, who taught Geography, was an old sweet-heart, the kindliest and gentlest member of that staff of sadists, snobs and incompetents. He was not to be spared, however. As a teacher, he was one of the enemy and we were out to get him.

George was jumpy and easily alarmed. Somebody told Tim Hurst that George had suffered shell-shock in the War. Demonically, he devised a plan to blast George out of his skin.

When George entered the classroom, we all lifted our desk lids by an inch. On a signal from Tim, we crashed them down and shouted 'BANG!' George fled to the staff-room. The deputy head, Mr Wilson, came down to us in a fury to announce that every boy in the class would be beaten if we did it again.

We ignored him. Our nerves were cool and battle-hardened by then. We knew that we could not be beaten so long as we acted together as one. Out of a group of nervous, eager, compliant children, anxious to please their teachers and willing to learn, Collyers had forged a cadre of dedicated trouble-makers. If our lives were to be made a misery, we would not, we determined, be the only ones to suffer.

9

Desmond Lynam was looking bulkier than I remembered. He probably would have thought the same of me if he had recognised me from our past. He was making a personal appearance at a trade show that I was visiting and I cornered him on a stand.

'You were at Varndean School in Brighton in the late 1950s and early 1960s, weren't you?' I said.

He looked suspicious. Perhaps he was wondering if I had been a victim of his bullying at school and was about to revenge myself by biffing his high-earning nose and messing up his moustaches.

'So?' he answered cautiously.

'Did you play cricket for the under-14 team?' I went on.

'Yes,' he said.

'Well then, I reckon you were probably one of my victims on the day I took seven Varndean wickets for nine runs playing for Collyer's School in Horsham.'

'Hah!' said Lynam, alert and interested now, all defences down. 'Was this at your place or ours?'

'Yours.'

'What, on that terrible strip of terraced ground the under-14s used to play on, with one boundary only about 30 yards from the stumps?'

'That's the one,' I said, excited to find that he was bringing memories back to me. 'The following year, I hit three sixes and four fours over that boundary out of an inning's score of 37.'

He laughed. 'Easy pickings, eh?' he said. We were mates now, greying and thickening old codgers recalling bright and brilliant days, more than 35 years ago, when each of us was 50 lbs lighter, our bodies were learning to do anything we asked of them and we were still supposing – no, we were certain – that we would soon be playing for England. In those moments with Lynam, it felt as if every second of my Collyer's cricketing summers of 1960 and 1961 had been made flesh again. I could feel again the sweat and the exhaustion of bowling unchanged for 18 overs and taking 8-24, including a hat-trick, on a blazing day and a perfect wicket in Midhurst. I could feel again that surging sense of exhilaration I shared with Mark Daniel and Martin Burgess and other members of the 1961 under-14s as we began to realise that ours was one of the best school teams in Sussex and that nobody was going to beat us easily. It all came back. I had a similar kind of moment, unearthing striated seams of memory of my Sussex boyhood, a couple of months ago when I was test-driving a sports' car on the old Goodwood circuit. The manufacturers had put an instructor in the cockpit to accompany me for some warm-up laps and guide me round the circuit. After a couple of laps during which he had been silent, the instructor said 'I feel a bit surplus to requirements out here.'

'I do know this track quite well,' I said. I could point to the spot where I saw Dan Gurney slide off the track in an F2 Porsche, one of the earliest rear-engined racing cars of the post-war era; there was the spot where I saw Bruce McLaren catch a 3.8 Jaguar saloon in a 360 degree spin; on this corner I saw Jim Clark in one of his first Lotus drives out brake and overtake Jack Brabham who was the master of the rear-engined Cooper; now we were passing the place where I saw Roy Bloxham's Lister-Jaguar leave the track, hit the bales, somersault, explode and toss Bloxham's blazing body on the grass like a broken doll.

'So you won't need me to tell you that over there,' he pointed away to a grassy knoll under a clump of trees, 'was where Stirling Moss had the massive shunt that ended his racing career in 1962.'

'I do know that,' I said. 'It was one of the worst days of my early life. It finished one of the happiest periods of my youth and I took no interest in motor racing for the next 25 years.' But it all came back that day on the track.

Cricket and motor racing were the matched obsessions of my early adolescence. West Sussex must have been as perfect a place for them to flourish as anywhere in England in the late 1950s and early 1960s. Lovely grounds, fine wickets, enthusiastic players, a county side that routinely gave more pleasure in losing matches with brio, flair, sometimes genius, than in winning championships, Sussex was the personification of a style and a manner of post-war cricket. Yorkshire were grim, stubborn and dreary. Surrey were professional, calculating, bloodless. Sussex was all step down the wicket, whack it over the sightscreen and let's go and have a pint while the sun's still shining. Call to mind the figure of Ted Dexter and you have the image of Sussex cricket.

Goodwood was Sussex cricket on wheels. Roy Salvadori, whom I watched at Goodwood at least ten times, spoke for me and for millions when he said 'Give me Goodwood on a summer day and you can forget the rest of the world.' Goodwood was blithe and gay just as those words were passing their age. It was also rapturous and careless in the mood of the Battle of Britain at the same time as it was cool, hip and jazzy. Goodwood was a confluence of the spirits of the ages, simultaneously Bentley-Barnato and Ferrari Dino. A day at Goodwood suggested that an adult life could be wonderful, thrilling and free and fun.

Going to Collyer's every day was like going to prison, punishing, humiliating, joyless. The teachers who unwillingly took my C stream recognised no special effort if it was made with school work, so my friends and I soon abandoned all effort. All my thoughts and all my energies, all my voracious reading, memorising, analysing and fantasising went into motor racing, jazz and cricket.

By the age of 14, I had become one of those pests with encyclopaedic knowledge who are dreaded by every car salesman. Drifting over to a Maserati 5000GT on the stand of the Motor Show at Earl's Court, I would ask a salesman whether the engine had ever been used in a race. When he said he didn't know, I would tell him that he ought to know that Carroll Shelby had raced it at Sebring. 'Go away, you little know-all,' he would hiss. Introduced to Don Lusher, a jazz trombonist, friend and client of my father's, I asked if he knew Bix Beiderbecke's 'Since My Best Gal Let Me Down'. When he said he couldn't remember, I sang him the whole number in a scat voice. 'Very impressive,' he sourly acknowledged.

Jazz and motor racing became corridors of escape that led away from the unhappiness of my school days and the increasing unhappiness of my home life. By 1960, my parents had become unable to conceal from their sons the strains in their marriage.

It struck me, for instance, that things might not be blissfully right between them when I came in one evening from cricket practice to find my father sitting on a kitchen chair with a piece of cauliflower on top of his head and a remote and glassy look in his eye. My mother was on her knees, mopping the kitchen floor and sobbing.

The story was that my father had come home late, his tie and the lapels of his jacket thrumming with scent. My mother had remonstrated. My brother had said 'Why don't you throw his dinner at him' and my mother had said 'I will' and did.

Moments like that made themselves felt. And the local tradesmen who were coming to the door, complaining that my father's cheques had bounced. And the bailiffs serving writs. And the rows all night and all through the weekend. While my parents raged at each other throughout a Sunday morning in the early summer of 1961, when I was 14, I slipped away to the bus shelter in Shermanbury with a packet of 10 tipped Admiral cigarettes and a copy of Motor Sport. And sat there for hours, smoking and reading, dwelling upon Dennis Jenkinson's thrilling account of Stirling Moss's victory over the shark-nosed Ferraris at Monaco and thinking 'It wouldn't be so bad to have Dennis Jenkinson's job if I can't be Stirling Moss' - an ambition I have come closer to fulfilling than Desmond Lynam has come to playing cricket for England.

Jazz and motor racing offered routes into adult life other than the miseries of monogamy and the drudgeries of school. Following them got me into trouble from the start. For one meeting at Goodwood in 1961, I travelled on the special Southdown coach from Horsham with a copy of Eddie Condon's jazz autobiography in my hand, a packet of Lucky Strike in my shirt pocket and a new pair of cavalry twill trousers touching new suede shoes. I felt as if I was Dave Brubeck crossed with Dave Charnley; but I was only 14, which was what I felt when the burning tip of a Lucky Strike came off in my hand and landed on a trouser leg, burning a hole in the cavalry twill that my mother had burst the bank to buy. Returned in that instant to panic-stricken infancy, I knew that I should have to lie to my mother, who would spot the burn as soon as she saw me (she did).

'It was an accident, Mum,' I was to say. 'I was talking to a man in the pits and he was waving his hand and his cigarette ash fell on me. I think he might have been Colin Chapman.' The lie needed to be simple though the embellishment could be grand.

But it was cricket that came first, mainly because I could do it. I couldn't play a musical instrument and I couldn't drive a car, but I could bowl and bat and catch and throw as well as any boy my age; so jazz and motor racing were recreational occupations for the times when I wasn't playing cricket.

Apart from giving me a lifelong hatred of snobs, especially teacher snobs, and of petty autocrats, especially teacher autocrats, and of self-satisfied moral imbeciles, especially the teacher kind, Collyer's School gave me nothing but cricket. It gave me cricket, however, in such delirious abundance that I almost feel grateful to the place.

The under-14 team was run by a teacher called David Brooshooft, a bachelor like almost half of the Collyer's staff, who dedicated long evenings and weekend afternoons to his team, which included a striking number of pretty little boys. No matter; those pretty little boys were terrific cricketers. Mark Daniel, our captain, had a genuine cricketing intelligence and was one of the very few captains I have ever played with who could think out another side. Martin Burgess, our wicket-keeper, was the best stumper and keeper of fast bowling I played with until I went to university.

Brooshooft was a real enthusiast and he made us a talented team. Every Tuesday evening in the winter term of 1961, he took us to Sussex County nets at Hove where we were coached by Jim Parks Senior and Junior, by Ted Dexter and, most usually, by a club professional named Cooper. He hated his job and disliked young boys, but Cooper got us playing straight, stretching our delivery strides, timing our half-volleys, moving our feet. He gave us technique. When the season began after Easter, we were better than our opponents by something like the measure that separates a county side from a good club team. We knew what we were doing. We were grooved.

I haven't got the school magazine, *The Collyerean*, for 1961. It went the way of all my other belongings when the family smash came, as it was soon to do; but, if I could look up the record now, I believe it would show that we won nearly all our games. We destroyed Hazelhurst. We blitzed Steyning. We took Midhurst to pieces. And as for Varndean . . .

'Wait a minute,' said Des Lynam (I was calling him Des by now). 'What years were you playing for Collyer's?'

'1961 and 1962.'

'Yes, well, you didn't get my wicket, brother. I was playing under-14 cricket in 1958 and 1959.'

'Don't tell me that,' I said. 'I've been telling the story for years about how I got you out first ball.'

'Well,' said Mr Lynam, turning away and terminating our brotherhood, 'I wouldn't want to ruin a good story with an awkward fact. You go on saying it if it suits you.'

Collyer's Under-14 team, 1961. The author, vice-captain, middle row, second left. Mark Daniel, captain, middle row, centre. Martin Burgess wicket keeper.

10

The first time I was thrashed by D.J. Coulson, headmaster of Collyer's School in Horsham, was in November 1959 when I was 13. I was a frightened little boy, so eager to do well at school that the shame of being caned by the Head was unbearable. As I waited my turn to enter his study, I was so panic-stricken that my legs were shaking and I could barely keep my stomach from throwing up. Begowned in his black academic robes and tightly knotted in his regimental tie, a darkly threatening figure, Coulson told me to lift my blazer and bend over. Then he lashed my buttocks six times with his bamboo cane.

The blows were so vicious that they knocked the breath out of my lungs. The bruises lasted for three weeks as they faded from black and red to blue, green and yellow. One of the weals was so livid, where his cane had struck twice on the same line of flesh, that speckles of blood were raised to the surface of the skin where it almost broke.

By the time of the second beating, 35 years ago as I am writing this, I had grown to be a tall, strong and bolshie-minded 15 year-old who was a mental inch away from refusing to submit to Coulson's cane and almost ready to knock him down. I took his whacks with fearless indifference, loathing that man with contempt for his brutal cruelty and, when he had finished, I stood up and walked out of his study determined that he would never do it again.

Those two beatings survive in my mind as more than vivid and separate occasions. They are a pair of mental bookends, marking the beginning and the end of a chapter of my boyhood in Sussex that feels like a continuous episode. The first caning was an indelible sign that, along with my friends from Cowfold, I was to be permanently marked among the C stream rejects and the trash in the bottom of the bin at Collyer's. The following two years continuously reinforced and confirmed that outcast branding. Meanwhile, during those two years, my family life at home descended into hell. The second beating coincided with the final crisis in my family and, together, they gave me a way out into a new life. When I walked out of Coulson's study that October morning in 1961, I expelled myself from that poxy school, with a dawning sense that whatever might be coming in the unknowable future it could not be worse than the years I had endured at Collyer's.

The story of the first beating is simple but it embodies a little more than local and limited interest. It touches on an ethical aspect of the corporal punishment debate that still continues in this country, for it raises the question whether the power to inflict brutal punishment should be given to teachers who may impose it arbitrarily, unjustly and malevolently. Does it do children good to receive undeserved and unfair punishment and to have no right of appeal? Is it a good lesson (it may be) for them to learn that adult authority may be capricious and irrational in its applications and sadistic in its motivations?

Along with my old friends from St Peter's C of E primary school in Cowfold, I travelled to Horsham to go to Collyer's on the Number 17 Southdown bus. Barry Austin, David Sawyer, Richard Keene, Peter Spedding, Tony Brookes, Stuart Faires and I sat together on the bus. I suppose that we were no better and no worse than any other group of schoolboys of that time: noisy, no doubt; always laughing at filthy thoughts; constantly scrounging dog-ends from each other; copying each other's homework - we must have got on the nerves of the other passengers who shared the bus, but I would not have thought that we ever exceeded the tolerance of those who remembered that they, too, were young once.

There was, however, a boy on the bus who was a sore pest, semi-psychopathic. His name was Ralph Lighten, known as Lightning. He went to the secondary modern school in Horsham and he drove us nuts. He fought and spat and screamed on every journey and attached himself to us regardless of the pastings we gave him to drive him away.

One morning at Assembly at Collyer's, Coulson read out all of our names, summoning us to his study after prayers. We looked at each other in horror and mystification, knowing that this was big trouble but clueless as to the cause. Coulson addressed us a group in his study. He had received a letter of complaint from a passenger on the bus, saying that a Collyer's boy had been blowing grains of dried rice through a pea-shooter around the bus's upper deck and that the passenger had suffered some painful hits.

Coulson declaimed our sentence like a black-capped High Court judge. He would not tolerate such conduct. He was not interested to know the identity of the perpetrator. We all shared responsibility for the offence. We had all blackened the school's name, so we must all suffer retribution.

Peter Spedding tried to tell Coulson about Lightning. He angrily refused to hear, saying that we were making it worse by trying to shift the blame. He told Tony Brooks to remain behind and sent the rest of us out of the room.

We stood in a line outside the door and listened as the cane whistled and cracked on Tony's behind. Peter Spedding said 'It will

This school photograph of 1960 shows the author *(second row, second from left)* **kneeling close to his tormentor, Collyer's headmaster D.J. Coulson** *(centre, without spectacles).*

only be three.' It was six. Stuart Faires and Barry Austin went absolutely white. I nearly wet myself.

My mother saw the weals on my buttocks when I was in the bath that weekend and she was appalled. What could I have done to deserve such a hiding? She was unconvinced by my story, as parents always rightly are when children protest their innocence. It was, in any case, an age of acquiescence as much for adults as for children. We did not question the authority (still less the probity) of doctors, policemen and teachers. Parents did not protest when their children were abused, even if they had been subjected to an assault which would be considered criminal today.

Besides, my parents had other things so much on their minds that my beating at school barely registered. Their gathering troubles were infinitely weightier and more painful than mine.

11

For 15 years, since the end of the war, my father had grown bored with his work as an accountant in London. Filling ledgers and filing returns for clients, no matter how glamorous and raffish they were, was a drudgery that he would always skip if he got the chance to play cricket or golf, to go to a boxing match or to the races. Constantly restless, always looking for the magical plan that would make him millions, he suffered from that fatal longing for the moment of thrilling transformation that would be sudden, total and forever. It led him into multiple flirtations, batty, hopeless schemes and, in the end, the most serious kind of trouble.

The fatal moment came around 1959, when he contrived to amalgamate his enthusiasms for easy money, dodgy characters and the ponies. With partners in London whom we never met and with a drinking companion on the Horsham-Victoria train named Peter Sumner-Moore, my old man cooked up a scheme called Fortunatus (the name alone crawls with low-life).

Fortunatus was a horse-race betting scam that depended upon the fathomless gullibility of punters. In essence, its pitch went like this: if you like a bet on the gee-gees, you will already know that the game is stitched up by its operators and that you, the ignorant outsider, are at the mercy of owners, trainers and jockeys who run the races to suit themselves. If you are going to win, you need to have inside information.

We are your friends at Fortunatus and we have the information. We are chummy with the owners, trainers and jockeys. We know where the fix is made. We know the horses that will lose and those that will win before they run. If you entrust us with your money, we will place your bets on your behalf and you will get your winnings, minus a consideration of 10% for our trouble.

That was the tenor and the tone of the advertisements my father and his crew placed in *The Sporting Life* and other learned tomes of the turf. Amazingly, they struck into a mother-seam of suckers. A tide of cash flooded through the mails into the ratty Oxford Street offices of Fortunatus, from whence it was borne around the corner to a betting office where my dad and his pals got a tidy commission from the bookies for bringing such healthy wads of boodle.

They made daily selections of horses and placed the punters' bets. Most, of course, lost. But some of them won, giving the partners a whacking share of the winnings.

For a time, my father was loaded. He bought a Mark VII Jaguar Saloon and a rack of natty suits for himself. He bought jewels and coats for my mother, furniture for the house and anything we wanted for his boys. He spread it around, not leaving out his ladies and his drinking chums on the train. He wanted everybody to have a good time and did not pause to count the cost.

As always, however, since his earliest manhood, he was spending more than he was earning. The legitimate returns from Fortunatus were lavish but they were insufficient. After a short sojourn in clover, my father and his mates needed more cash and they were beginning to run out of suckers. It dawned on them – this must have been late in 1960 – that, since most of their selected nags duly lost and the punters forfeited their cash, they might as well not wager the money at all but keep it in their pockets.

This, certainly, was an even more profitable approach and tidy in its simplicity but it had the defect of being an outright crime. It was Fraud, Embezzlement, Misappropriation – all in capitals.

At home, of course, we knew none of this. We only knew that the old man who had always been such good fun had become peevish, irritable and argumentative. He bickered constantly, blazingly, with my mother and with his sons. He drank. He was always late. He forgot my birthday in 1960. He became a lousy father. He was going to pieces. In the summer of 1961, my parents sold our house in Shermanbury and we moved to a rented house in Roffey on the outskirts of Horsham. My father had told my mother that the money from the house would clear his debts and get him out of trouble. It was wishful thinking. Or a lie. Probably both.

On a Friday afternoon early in October 1961, I rode my bike home to Roffey from Collyer's to find that my father had already returned from London. He and my mother were in the sitting room which was as still as a morgue. My mother was crying and there were dry lines of tears on my father's face.

They had to tell me that the jig was up. My father said that he had been under police investigation for more than a year. He had paid thousands in bribes to a detective constable at West End Central to stave off prosecution but he had now been told he would be arrested. He was certain to be imprisoned.

We talked most of the evening and the following Saturday morning. My mother was determined to flee from Horsham and go to live with one of her sisters, either in Essex or in Salisbury. She said that we should change our name to avoid the disgrace that would come when my father's trial was covered in the newspapers. The case was bound to get attention because he had defrauded some of his famous clients, such as Alan Freeman.

'Are you saying that I shall have to leave Collyer's?' I asked in despair. Knowing nothing better, and even though I had never been valued there, I loved that school, chiefly for my friends and for cricket. I could not, at that moment, imagine a life beyond Collyer's. My father wept as he said that I would have to leave. I pleaded with him to think of an alternative. Perhaps I could stay with a family in Horsham and continue at Collyer's. My father was reluctant, saying that my mother would need me to be with her; but he offered to go and see Coulson. He went to the school that afternoon and told Coulson the whole story.

He returned to say that Coulson had refused any help and had said that I must leave the school. My father was obviously stunned by the hardness of this rejection but was too demoralised to argue.

I went to school on Monday morning carrying a letter in my pocket from my father in which he told Coulson that I would be leaving the school as soon as we had somewhere to go. I was in a daze. In the lower parade ground, by the old bomb-shelters, I told my friends Dennis Strudwick, Tim Hart and Kurt Holt - the rapscallions of the C stream who had become my brothers in trouble-making - that my time at the school was finishing. They were shocked and wanted to know more while the rest of the school gathered in the hall for Assembly.

We went into one of the bomb-shelters and went on talking, to be discovered by a patrolling master, O'Connor the maths' teacher. He flew into a rage, said that we were smoking (for once, we were not) and sent us to the headmaster.

Coulson gave us a viciously excoriating lecture, saying that we were all delinquents and on the verge of expulsion. This would be our last chance to mend our ways, and we would all be caned.

I remember that as we stood outside, waiting our turns, Tim and Kurt were careless. I apologised for getting them into trouble. 'Don't worry about that,' said Tim. 'It's nothing.'

Coulson did not speak to me when I entered his study except to say 'Bend over'. I looked back and up at him, with a kind of quizzical indifference, as he raised the cane and the wings of his black gown opened. I stood still to take the hits, feeling no pain. When he had finished, I stood up, took my father's letter out of my blazer pocket and said 'This is for you.'

The corridors and the hall were empty and silent as I walked through them. The school was at its lessons and the voices of the teachers droned distantly. I went to the bicycle sheds, took out my Phillips Fleur de Lys and rode away down Hurst Road without looking back. My mother was outraged when I told her what had happened.

'He beat you!' she exclaimed, 'even though he knew what a mess we're in. Well, that's it: you're never going back to that school.'

The following Saturday, we did a bunk, leaving Sussex forever. My father borrowed a Morris 1000 Traveller from one his drinking cronies on the train and we filled it with cases and boxes and a divan bed. I lay on that bed for the journey, with my feet sticking through the double doors where they were tied together. My mother wore her best fur hat and sat in the front seat while my father drove through a golden autumn morning along the roads from Sussex to Hampshire and Wiltshire and my aunt Mabel and uncle Charlie's bungalow in Salisbury.

On the way, I composed for myself a new identity, a new self. I was ready to be a proper teenager, sexy and wild, rather than continuing as the tubby and neuter, obedient and quiescent boy whose days I was glad to feel were ended.

I imagined a new life for myself in which I would get a job outside of school hours and go my own way. I would wear tight jeans and go to jazz clubs. I would smoke and drink and have love affairs and read what I liked. A clear idea dawned on my mind of a future life, much of which was actually to become true.

For this new life and this new personality, post-Sussex and post-Collyer's, I already had been given a new name. My mother had decided that, in Salisbury, we would be known by her maiden name of Lyndon. That has been my name for 35 years.

Until that October day in 1961 and throughout my Wealden boyhood, my name had been Neil Barnacle.

The author today.

EPILOGUE

'This is Heartland to me and always will be,' said my son John the other day, as we drove into the Suffolk village where he was born, only four miles from where I now live. 'I feel as if I know every stone and branch here.'

I feel the same about the Weald between Brighton and Horsham, even though I have never lived there since October 1961 and probably never shall again. My attachment to that area is indelible and permanent.

My work occasionally takes me somewhere near the Weald and, invariably, I find myself drawn there, even if it is more than 50 miles out of my way. I drive the roads around Henfield, Shermanbury, Partridge Green, Cowfold and Lower Beeding. I lurk in the churchyard of St Peter's in Cowfold and tread the same flagstones I trod as a child along the path to the gates of the village school. I walk the banks of the ponds and rivers I fished and pace the football fields and cricket pitches where I learned to play the games I still love.

Writing the series of articles for *Downs Country* contained in this book gave me the chance to live again, in memory, in that Heartland.

The stories in these pages are unlike any I have written since I first began to sell my work nearly 30 years ago. They are the only ones I have ever written for no pay. They are the only ones I have been given a free hand to write as the fancy took me, without any direction or messing-about from an editor. And they are the only ones I have written without any idea or sense of a readership. I wrote them for myself, for no other reason than that I had always I wanted to get these stories out of my mind and my memory. The opportunity, the reason to write, never came my way until I met Colin Dunne.

Founder, editor, publisher, architect-in-chief and principal tea-bag masher of *Downs Country*, Colin Dunne gave me the chance to write this series of articles soon after we first met in 1994. He had told me about the magazine and I had told him that I had spent my boyhood in the heart of *Downs Country*. Would he let me have a go at writing about that time? I could never get him to see that he was giving me a unique privilege and an immense favour.

Writing these stories for *Downs Country* gave me a licence not just to indulge my own habitual ransacking of memory but to tie together parts of my life that had been violently smashed apart. I knew the last line of this series before I wrote the first word but, until I came to the moment, I had not written out the name I was given at birth for 35 years. There was a humpty-dumptyish feeling of pasting together the broken pieces of a past in the writing of these pages.

Beyond that strange process, the series also put me in touch with my lost life in tangible reality. Trevor Adcock, who comes into the story about my father's cricketing at Henfield, was in touch with Colin Dunne after the article appeared. As the keeper of the club records that Pam compiled, he even found my own and my brother's names in the ledgers as junior members. He was also quick to confirm to Colin that my father had, indeed, been a handy cricketer; and this was reinforced by other readers who wrote kindly to say that they vividly remembered my father's batting. It was marvellous to hear from them.

When Ann Burrell - my inamorata from St Peter's in Cowfold - wrote to me after the last article of the series had been published in March 1997, her letter was the first material connection I had had with my Sussex years for half a lifetime. Its impact was so powerful that it made me feel dizzy. Ann's letter came from Palo Alto in California where she now works as a toxicologist for IBM, having got a degree in botany and a doctorate in biochemistry. An old friend from Horsham High School had sent her copies of *Downs Country*.

Ann and I wrote long letters to each other, comparing memories of that time and filling in the years between. In November 1997, we met for dinner in London. Both past our own half-centuries, we spent most of the evening talking about our children.

We were both fascinated to find that our memories of the time we had shared were so different and that each of us had recollections which stirred separate memories in the other. Ann corrected some slipshod mistakes I had made in the early writing and I also discovered that, while I had affectionate, almost loving feelings towards Old Slokie, she was still peeved with him for his oddities as a teacher. I had forgotten, until Ann crisply reminded me, that Slokie would orate for hours about the escape adventures of PoWs in German camps. She, it was obvious, had not enjoyed these sagas as much as I had; nor had she entirely forgiven me for wasting so much of the class's time by prompting Slokie into telling them. She also made me feel that I had not given enough credit to Mr Squires in my stories about St Peter's. He, we agreed, was the teacher who first made us feel that we could do good things.

Ann told me that her earliest experiences at Horsham High School for Girls tallied with mine and my boy contemporaries at Collyer's. Like us, she had found herself at sea in subjects, like languages, where other children had already made a start at prep and private schools. Unlike us, she had encountered no snootiness among the teachers towards the 'Cowfold clods', as we were known at Collyer's. Instead, she had benefited from encouragement and sympathetic teaching as her subsequent success testifies.

The words 'Cowfold clod' came back at me across the decades from an angry correspondent who wrote to Colin Dunne at *Downs Country* to denounce my articles about my Collyer's years. The writer, staunchly sticking up for his old school and its Headmaster D.J. Coulson, said that, as a Cowfold clod, I had shown myself to be intellectually and morally unworthy of that noble institution.

A suggestion that he might have been wrong and that Collyer's was, indeed, the pile of snobberies, incompetencies, cruelties and worse that I remembered came from David Sawyer. We knew him as 'Dod' at St Peter's in Cowfold. He had joined Collyer's in the same year as me. Through the tenacious digging of Ann Burrell, Dod and I were connected with each other and talked on the telephone.

Dod had stayed in Horsham, had gone on playing football for Cowfold into middle age, had kept in touch with many of my childhood friends. Colin Sparks, he told me, had just retired from the police force. Beryl Smith was teaching in Steyning. Doug Barrett, our friend in Cowfold who was always horse-crazy, had appallingly been killed in a race when he was in his early twenties, having already made a name for himself as a professional jockey. More happily, Dod and I remembered the ravishing Janice Hawkins with the same undying ardour.

Dod did not need to remind me that he had made his way out of the C streams at Collyer's, reaching the A streams in the third and fourth years. What had happened then, I asked? He had, he said, been pushed beyond his limits, had not done well in O levels and, feeling dispirited, had left school as soon as he could.

Dod was no less gifted than I was nor, I would say, than Ann Burrell. After I left Collyer's, I went to a school where I got the same kind of attention and encouragement as Ann received at Horsham High School. She went to university. I went to university. David Sawyer could also have gone to university if he had wanted to and if he had gone to a decent school.

The correspondence columns of *Downs Country* went on buzzing with letters about Collyer's long after my series of articles ended. Many correspondents complained that the school and its staff had been unfairly defamed. They should have heard my conversation with Dod in which he reminded me of strangenesses among the staff there that I had not included in my stories. One episode, in which Coulson monstrously alleged sexual misconduct among a group of our friends, was so perverse, so malignant, that Dod was hesitant about reminding me, even after 35 years. We remembered other teachers whose interest in the boys would have had them arraigned by Esther Rantzen today. The more I think about that place, the more I abhor it. Neither time nor distance have mellowed the sourness I feel for Collyer's and at least a dozen of the men who taught there.

Bitterness should have little place in these final thoughts, however. I have told these stories about the responses that came from my articles in order to show how, miraculously, the opportunity that Colin Dunne gave me to write about my own personal past stirred up a mass of interconnections among a host of people, many unknown to each other. Having no sense of a readership when I was writing, I found myself connected to a society through publication.

I want to thank all those who wrote to me and to the magazine following the articles. The letters we received filled in the gaps in a history that was local and general as well as being personal and particular. One of my favourites came from a lady who was sure she had found me out in making up the whole thing. She had worked in the soft drinks industry after the War, she wrote, and she could say definitely that there had been no such thing as a can of 7-Up in the mid-Fifties, when I remembered buying one for the first time while watching my father playing cricket for Henfield. I must be an impostor.

No, madam, just mistaken. It must have been a bottle, not a can. I have corrected that mistake in this book, along with others that have been pointed out to us. The discovery of each more accurate detail, each deeper truth, has been as great a pleasure as the writing itself. Thanks to everyone who came along on this journey and found something in it for themselves.

Neil Lyndon
May, 1998

Six of the best

Many readers of *Downs Country* found themselves moved to write to the magazine about the memories stirred by Neil Lyndon's serialised *Boyhood*. Most letters were warmly appreciative ('I did shed a tear over the last article,' one confessed), but the author's loathing for Collyer's School proved hotly controversial. We here reprint half a dozen responses.

I had to write to you to protest about the article in your last issue about Collyer's School. I was at the school at about the same time and I must say that my memories bear no resemblance whatsoever to his - I can hardly think we went to the same establishment.

Certainly, the discipline was strict and boys were caned, but I always found the staff to be skilful teachers who were always willing to give up their time to help any of the boys.

I firmly believe that the traditional education which gave boys a clear set of guidelines turned out generations of well-educated, well-balanced, responsible and civilised men.

When I see some of the youngsters being turned out by the comprehensives today, I dearly wish there were more schools of that type.

D.R. Brown, Brighton

Cowfold cowboy Neil Lyndon 's article about Collyer's grammar school was seditious.

As a graduate of 'Ma' Young's 1956 class of 1c, my boyhood impressions of this fine institution and its teachers were congenial.

As for the regimental ties and scholastic gowns, their finery commanded respect by example. The classroom eccentricities and alleged shortcomings of 'Froggy' Kenyon, 'Mungo' Park and other teachers were pleasant diversions during a rich educational experience. To decry the staff as second-raters and duds could come only from a Cowfold country clod.

My Collyer's career progressed from almost bottom of 1c to 6A, despite a caning by the 'venomous' Coulson, who subsequently made me a gold-tasselled prefect.

No, Mr Lyndon, Collyer's did not forge a cadre of dedicated trouble-makers. It moulded players and leaders.

Michael J. Ansell, Ontario, Canada

I write to object to the nasty little article by Neil Lyndon. I do so as someone related to one, and acquainted with several, of the members of staff at Collyer's School who put years of devotion into maintaining the school tradition as one of enviable excellence and opportunity for those willing to learn. My Lyndon seems to have failed to appreciate any of the benefits of even a partially selective system.

Yes, the C stream did contain some who were, rightly or wrongly, castigated as 'thick'. It also contained those who were actually or potentially unpleasant or disruptive. By the time they had reached 3c they had been given every opportunity to reject or revel in these judgements. Sadly Mr Lyndon appears to be one who has not grown out of any of them.

Not having had the misfortune to teach him, it is not for me to comment on his literary style. As to learning another language, it may be that he fell into the category described by another teacher in another school, in a pupil's report: 'He seems to regard it as very unfair that he is expected to learn another language when he clearly hasn't mastered his own.'

A nasty little article, whichever way you look at it - or him!

Peter C. Benner, Warninglid

How timely that you should be publishing Neil Lyndon's moving and horrifying account of his schooldays at Collyer's at exactly the time when corporal punishment is once again under discussion.

Caning, I believe, has its place as a school punishment, so long as it is civilised with restraint, caution and judgement. Like Mr Lyndon, I, too, experienced Coulson's beatings which had, as I recall, none of these qualities.

M. Davies, Dorking

Neil Lyndon's article horrified me. I attended Collyer's from 1949 to 1954 when the head was the long-serving P.A. Tharp.

For all his odd ways, P.A.T., as he was generally known, was a reasonably fair man who really did want all of his charges to benefit from his school's offerings. Like all heads of those times, he did beat boys who had badly offended; but never did I hear that he had caused the kind of injuries that his far less illustrious successor appears to have inflicted.

To understand the underlying reason for D.J. Coulson's excesses, it is necessary to realise that he was an ambitious man. He was using Collyer's as a stepping stone to better things - getting a headship at a Headmasters' Conference School. What horrifies me about the man is that SIX strokes of the cane seem to have been his norm. Such a punishment was only ever intended for use as a last resort. Was there a witness to his brutal use of the cane? Full-blown state schools had to have any caning witnessed by another master. What was put in the punishment book? All canings had to be registered in detail; it would be most interesting to inspect Collyer's punishment book for that time, so see what was put into it.

The staff at Collyer's during my time there were some of the most important and endearing people that have ever entered my life. Their names, faces and the very sounds of their voices still ring clear and true. That the world which had been cultured with such care by P.A. Tharp should have been so adulterated by an over-ambitious man was a terrible tragedy. I am so sorry that Neil Lyndon did not experience the real Collyer's of earlier years.

A.I.E. Booker, Barns Green, near Horsham

Neil Lyndon's article about being beaten at Collyer's evoked very strong emotions because it brought back vivid memories of my own beatings at the school in the late Forties and early Fifties. It was a shock to read that Collyer's headmaster was still beating boys as late at 1961; in a valid discussion about corporal punishment, an individual's hurt is so clearly remembered after all these years.

My beatings were administered by Coulson's predecessor, P.A. Tharp. I was something of a protégé of his, and yet he seemed to think it right to give me 'six of the best' on three occasions: for dangling a small boy on a rope over a banister outside 'Froggy' Kenyon's room, for breaking the largest pane of glass in the school and for refusing (as a spectator) to retrieve a cricket ball that had gone over the boundary.

It is possible that I deserved punishment for the first two offences (though not that sadistic thrashing) but even Tharp, I am still convinced, knew he had no justification whatsoever for the third beating. I am glad Neil Lyndon's article was published.

Unlike him, I would not call Collyer's a 'poxy school', as I value my academic years. But I resent to this day the regime of control and culture of compulsion. It was the source, I am sure, of my lifelong resistance to authority and conformity.

Michael Horan, East Grinstead

Footnote: After leaving Collyer's, Neil Lyndon went on to a comprehensive school in Dorset, passing 11 O-levels and three A-levels and later taking a degree in English at Cambridge.

DOWNS
COUNTRY

If you have enjoyed Neil Lyndon's story, you're sure to enjoy DOWNS COUNTRY - the magazine in which it first appeared as a series of articles.

DOWNS COUNTRY, which is published six times a year, is a traditional countryside magazine for Sussex, Kent, Hampshire and Surrey. In its pages you will find high-class writing and beautiful illustrations, history, heritage and humour, wildlife, walks and nostalgia. It is a celebration of life in the south, past and present.

The magazine is available in most newsagents, but if you would like a free copy to see for yourself, all you have to do is write to DOWNS COUNTRY, Freepost SCB2547, Midhurst, West Sussex GU29 0BR, and we'll send you one.